New Plains Review Fall 2020

New Plains Review Fall 2020

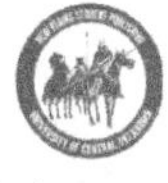

New Plains Student Publishing University of Central Oklahoma

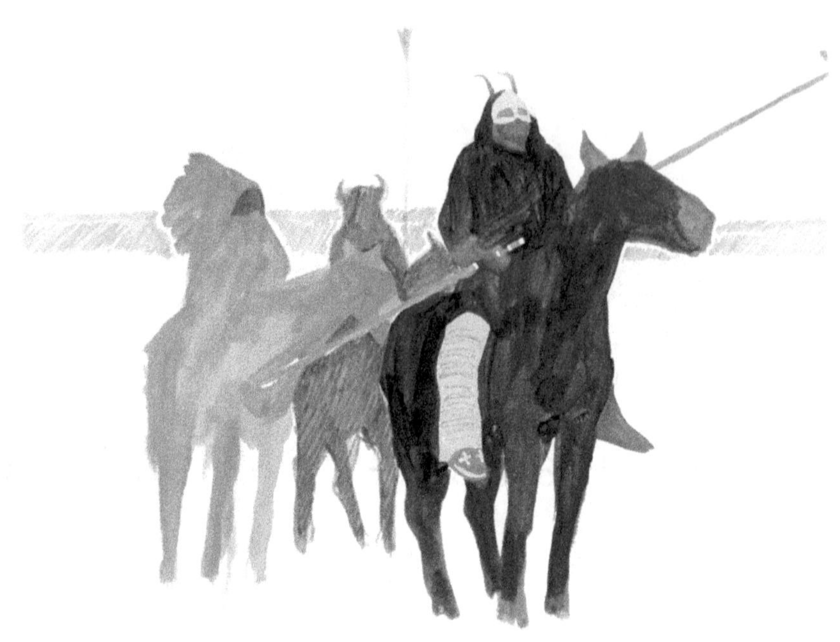

Phantom Warriors
Sherman Chaddlesone

NEW PLAINS REVIEW is edited by students and faculty of the English Department in the College of Liberal Arts at the University of Central Oklahoma. The political, social, or artistic commentary represents the views of the writers and artists, and inclusion in the journal does not indicate editorial endorsement or non-endorsement.

New Plains Review does not claim to represent the views of the University or its officials.

The image found on the previous page is from a painting titled Phantom Warriors by acclaimed Native American artist and UCO alumnus Sherman Chaddlesone.

Visit our website at newplainsreview.com

Email inquiries to newplainsreview @ gmail.com

English Department, Box 184
University of Central Oklahoma
100 North University Drive
Edmond, Oklahoma 73034

Published in the USA; printing & manufacturing information can be found on the final page.

CONTENTS

A Peculiar Day in the Douro Valley   1

Cornerstone   17

Escaping the Party   26

Floyd and the Magic Spectacles   33

Hunting The Sacred Animal, Two Rivers 1916   49

Into the Frame   58

Off Broadway   66

One More Hug   77

Spring   90

David Drake   93

The Line: A Play in One Act   95

Three Paintings by Edward Hopper   114

nightmares that formed me   117

CONTENTS

Backpacking 119

Haughty 121

Road Map 123

Fishermen 125

American Songs 127

Pine Cones 129

AI News 131

Window Seat 136

November; The Skier; The Subway 138

EMULSION 142

Remember 143

BUYING THE REAL: THE 1950S 145

Strawberries 147

The Event 150

HELICOPTERS, HURRICANES, CAR WRECKS! 151

Lost Falcon 153

BIOGRAPHIES 157

A Peculiar Day in the Douro Valley

BENJAMIN LITOFF

Paco sat outside his cottage with the vines that grew in his terrace dangling above him. He sipped his espresso as the morning sun rose over Pinhao. The Douro Valley labor harvested the grapes in the morning before the summer heat rose to unbearable temperatures. Even this early in the day, Paco wore his shirt unbuttoned, his bare chest breathing the valley air. The hairs on his chest stood up.

The hills alternated between green and brown, and portrayed various textures depending on the time of day or the direction he looked. Clumps of trees scattered across the hills bore ripe dates. Paco enjoyed watching the automobiles as the drivers cut the wheels to make the sharp turns on the valley roads.

This was Paco's second year in Pinhao. His cottage was rustic, isolated, and, to his liking, intimate. He had a minimalist approach to the interior, since he had only brought a few of his possessions over from Oviedo. Nothing he owned, however, predated the Civil War. There was nothing he kept from his childhood in northern Spain other than his memories of running through the streets near the Cathedral of San Salvador. His identity was not cultivated from childhood but born from the blood, bones, and intestines that he witnessed scattered across grass and stone.

Inside, he kept his uniform from the war in a locked trunk with the exception of his boots that he placed to the side. His rifle had no ammunition; he kept it as a memento. But, his pistol always had a full magazine ready to be cocked to load a bullet in the chamber. Those firearms came into his possession when the Siege of Oviedo began and they served him until Franco won the war.

Paco's most cherished possession that he brought from Spain dwarfed the value he designated to his wartime relics. During the years when the wars, that would dictate the successes and failures of ambitious empires, were beginning to dwindle, and as citizens of the world witnessed climaxes featuring the final falling bombs and the fading echoes of flying bullets, Paco found his best friend.

Humo ran from inside and snuggled against Paco's leg. Humo's beige hair curled like springs on a springboard and hid his wild eyes. The white on his chest resembled spilled paint. Saliva dripped from his dangling tongue as he panted.

Paco acquired Humo from a farmer who specialized in breeding Spanish Water Dogs who herd sheep. While Paco had no sheep to herd—his only other animal was a horse named Alfonso—he admired the grace and athleticism of the canine breed. They were short with goofy hair, like a child whose parents neglected to groom, but there was a nobility to them. They moved with agility and kept their heads held up with a confidence that was more common to Bengals and Cobras or other predators who had wicked abilities to hunt and maul their prey.

"It is too hot today," Humo said. "This is the hottest day I can remember."

"You said that yesterday," Paco told his dog.

"I don't remember saying that."

Humo nuzzled his snout against Paco's foot. He reached down and stroked Humo's back; the dog's curls popped up from under his palm and between his fingers.

"I am going down into town later. Is there anything you want me to bring back?"

"Yes, Guardián. There is something you can do for me," Humo said. He looked up from where he had rested his head, but he couldn't meet his eyes due to the hair obstructing his face. "You can bring me the corpse of that vulgar vulture."

Paco rolled his eyes. Humo had claimed he saw an Egyptian Vulture a few days ago. While native to the Iberian Peninsula, Paco didn't believe that Humo saw one in the valley so close to the Douro River.

Paco stood up and began buttoning his shirt. His hair was already combed and he decided to keep his five o'clock shadow cast over his face for the day. In the silence of the valley, he took a final sip of his morning espresso and he could hear the hands of his watch tick as he brought his wrist up near his face.

"It is unlikely that I will be able to bring you that bird when I return."

"I see. Well, Guardián, I will make a promise to you. I will slay that vile scavenger and I will bring its carcass to your feet as a worthy tribute."

"Why so much animosity for that bird?"

"It's a repugnant thing. I once saw it eat dung."

"So? I've seen you eat dung."

Humo huffed. "One time that happened."

Paco rode Alfonso down the dirt roads, where he could roll down for what would seem like eternity if his horse decided to buck and throw him from the saddle. The prospect of falling did not frighten Paco, who flew SM.81s during the war. He had flown over Barcelona alongside the Legionary Air Force. If flying a mechanical vehicle from thousands of feet in the air did not frighten Paco, a horse on a narrow valley would not either.

Whenever he looked down the valley, and across the river, at the brown and green hills, he thought of Barcelona. The sight reminded him of the city's grid when he looked out the window as his plane soared. He saw the debris and smoke gather in clumps. Even though he was right over the city, it felt as if he was leagues away. The sounds from the explosion could barely reach him. He was so far removed from the cacophony of war. He was too high up in the clouds to hear the chaos of wailing widows crying beside maimed men as they attempted to save the lives of now crippled children.

After the first barrage, Paco spoke with the same men who had educated him on the SM.81s controls. They had always been polite to him with their instructions and were patient as they tried to navigate the language barrier between their native Italian and his Spanish. Paco described the noises he heard and the Italians in the platoon told him that his description was identical to their experience in Guernica.

Those memories stayed with Paco until he reached the town and hitched his horse outside Rufete Restaurante, where the white awning contrasted with the name written in black. He took off his hat and fanned his clammy face and sweat-drenched pits before walking through the door. The clamoring inside among friends, with the tapping of silverware against plates that held local delicacies, was louder to him than bombs. This was a pleasant oasis for him.

Patricia, the owner's daughter, was hosting as she normally did. She recognized everyone from town, including Paco. They exchanged platonic pecks on each cheek as they greeted each other. She had always been patient with Paco's imperfect Portuguese.

"You didn't bring the silly rascal with you?" she asked.

"I left him at home. He was being a bit chatty today."

Patricia laughed. "He's always trying to tell us something and gets irritated when we don't listen."

Paco was ready to take his seat at his usual table under the black and white framed photograph of women stomping on grapes. He was ready to order the Mariscada with a perfect pairing of white wine that was harvested just half a mile away. But before he could go on with the routine, Patricia gripped his arm.

"These two Germans came by looking for you. An older, married couple."

"Germans here?" Paco asked. "What happened? Were all the flights from Berlin to Brazil booked?"

"They specifically asked for you."

"For me?"

Patricia nodded. She seemed to anticipate Paco's next question, and told him she did not know why they inquired for him.

"They are staying at the inn just a few doors down," she said. "At least, that is what they told me. They ate here and left about fifteen minutes ago."

"Maybe I can catch them," Paco said. "Excuse me, please. My apologies, darling."

Paco ran outside and past Alfonso. He knew which inn Patricia referred to and he also knew the proprietors and the workers. When he opened the door the bell dinged.

"Excuse me, sir," he said to the man behind the counter. "I don't mean to pry or make a request of you that would leave you in a position to make an unprofessional decision, but I heard an older German couple is inquiring about my whereabouts."

The clerk smiled. "Ah, yes. The Schmitzs. They were asking about you. I believe they may have looked up your address in the directory."

"Do you know when they will be back?"

"They won't. They checked out already."

Paco left the inn. He was hungry but dumbfounded by the idea of Germans looking for him. He had not even seen a German since the thirties. Not since he left Spain.

Still bewildered, Paco mounted Alfonso and rode back to his cottage without eating. He did not rush on his travels back, but he did not idle either. This was the first time he traveled on these roads without the memories of Barcelona clinging to his thoughts.

He came home expecting the German couple to be waiting for him. No one was there. Just Humo patrolling outside sniffing about. When he saw Paco he ran over with his rear end wagging with vigor.

"Guardián, I kept the house secure."

"Humo, did any Germans come by here looking for me?"

"Germans? Why would they be here? Were all the flights to Brazil booked?"

Paco let out an abrupt, quick laugh. "Ha! I made that same joke."

The morning ended and still no German couple came to his door. Paco made breakfast and fed Humo. Whatever fish he didn't finish he placed on the floor for Humo to devour. It was not until he watched Humo eat that he realized he did not pray before his meal. A crucifix hung beside his door and he looked at the symbol as he made the sign of the cross and kissed his knuckle.

A mirror hung above the sink, right beside the window that looked out towards the valley. As he washed his plates, his eyes darted back and forth from the vines growing in the hills to his own reflection.

"What do you think of this little bit of facial hair?" he asked Humo.

"You look handsome with that scruff."

"I am not sure. I might shave it."

"You will look handsome clean-shaven."

"During the war, I had a mustache. I might regrow that."

"You will look handsome with a mustache."

Paco turned around and bent down to stroke Humo's snout. His entire rear wagged as his legs bounced. Humo's panting breath hit Paco's face. The hot air made his perspiration worse and so he slid off his unbuttoned shirt onto the floor.

"Outside! Outside!" Humo shouted as he adjusted and shifted his ears. "Something is outside!"

Paco looked through the kitchen window. A man and a woman stood outside with the wineries in the backdrop. Their charcoal clothes were an ugly contrast to all the vibrant green around them. Looking at their clothes made Paco feel uncomfortably hot. Beside them was a duffel bag.

The couple stood shoulder to shoulder, their height was identical. Their hair was the same shade of gray with whorls of black, even though the woman appeared younger. When Paco stepped outside, they smiled and waved at him with familiarity. Neither the man or the woman seemed bothered by Humo's howl that echoed from the house.

"Greetings, friend," the man called out. His German accent was prominent. "Pardon us. I hope we are not interrupting your afternoon. We are new to the area and were looking for a friend."

"Are we friends?" Paco asked. "My apologies if my memory is failing me. I don't know many Germans."

"Please forgive our rudeness for not introducing ourselves. This is my wife, Erika Schmitz. And I am Benno, of Berlin. You may have known our son, Ernst."

Humo ran out the door with his tail straight back and his snout pointing forward.

"Tell those Nazis to get lost," Humo hollered.

"That is a beautiful canine," Erikah complimented.

"Your flattery is wasted on me." He looked up and glared at Paco through the curls that covered his eyes. "Say the word and I'll tear them apart."

Paco reached into his pocket and pulled out a pack of cigarettes. He put one to his lips and patted his pockets for matches. Humo began yelling at his guardian to watch out, but Paco did not see Benno approach the two of them. Benno had reached into his pocket and pulled out what looked like the grip of a pistol. Paco froze, with the cigarette stuck hanging from his dry lips.

Benno held a light in his hands, the metal case the size of a stone. The flame stood upright, like a soldier in formation before a march. Paco leaned his head forward and listened to the sizzle of his now lit smoke. Engraved into the metal, Paco noticed the swastika.

Similar to a slight of hand trick, Benno put the light back in his jacket pocket and pulled out a newspaper clipping, a seamless switch of the two objects.

"Is this you?" Benno asked.

Paco grabbed the parchment. The paper had browned and it reminded Paco of rotting flesh. The black ink was difficult to read over the darkened paper, but with squinted eyes he could still make out the story.

The author wrote in Spanish and used adjectives like brave and resilient in the text below the headline that contained Paco's name.

"Is that you they're talking about in the paper?" Benno asked again.

"Yes," Paco admitted. "Do you two want to come in for a drink? I have some wine."

"That would be lovely," Erikah said. "Wine is perfect for a hot day like this one."

Paco stepped to the side and ushered the couple into his home. They walked in, as if the place was familiar to them. They did not hesitate.

"I don't trust them, Guardián," Humo said. "Haven't you read of all the awful things they have done?"

"Have I read them?" Paco asked, insulted by the audacity. "Yes, I read them. I read them to *you* because *you* are an illiterate."

"Now you're just being hurtful!"

Paco bent down and grabbed Humo by the back of the neck. "I need you to relax. Everything is okay."

Humo sighed. "Okay. I trust you, Guardián."

The couple sat at the table while Paco refilled two dwindling glasses of port wine. They had many questions for Paco, and Paco had many questions as well. He was intrigued by their presence in a country whose government, while neutral for most of the war, ultimately ended up siding with the Allies. Benno drank his wine with haste, while Paco sipped his. Erikah declined a glass, despite noting earlier that wine would be perfect for a hot day.

Erikah picked up Paco's shirt from the floor and handed it to him when he walked inside. She had already placed their duffel bag beside the front door. Paco sat down, then slipped the shirt on and fastened the buttons from the top down. Benno's suit jacket hung on the back of his chair, revealing a holstered pistol under his armpit.

"So, mister and miss Schmitz...what makes you think I would know your son, Ernst?"

Before he had even asked this first question, Benno was already halfway finished with his second glass of wine.

"Have you heard of the name Hugo Sperrle?"

"Of course. He was...how do you say it in Germany? A generalfeld-marschall?" Paco asked, butchering the pronunciation.

"And what else do you know of this man?" Benno asked.

Paco peered over at Humo, who was sitting in front of the couch, watching them intensely. His ears were up and his rear was off the floor, ready to spring into action if needed. He mirrored the demeanor his guardian was able to keep hidden from the guests.

"I am ignorant in my knowledge of German army officials," Paco admitted.

"We had a son serve under him in the Great War when Hugo was a Hauptamann...how do you say that in Spanish? Capitán, I believe?"

Paco nodded, even though he was not sure if that was true or not. "Was this Ernst who had fought in this war?"

"No," Erikah said. "We had three sons. Walter served in the Great War."

"I owned a factory that did decently," Benno interrupted. "My family had always been loyal to the empire and the war efforts." He paused to finish his wine in one gulp. He held out his glass and Paco refilled. Benno continued as the purple wine splashed in the glass. "When his plane was shot down by the British, it devastated us. They told us it would be best not to look at our son's corpse for it was so mangled and burned in the crash."

Humo rested his rear on the wood floor. He sensed Paco's anxiety wither and give rise to sympathy. Humo's ears flopped down as he leaned backwards against the cushions.

"Times were hard after that. Not just for us but for the country," Erikah said. "It seemed like we were losing money everyday. At times we had to forgo meals. That is the only reason why we did not protest when Ernst joined the military. He had an opportunity to build a career during his service and we supported him."

"And Ernst, he fought in Spain?" Paco asked.

"Let me ask you a question," Benno said.

Paco did not even see Benno finish his glass of port wine. He held it out again, like a rude customer who hurried the waiter. Paco filled the glass again with the last drops from the bottle. The purple stained Benno's lips and teeth; it looked as if he had smudged lipstick.

"Why did you choose to fight for Franco?"

While Paco never received this question before, he already knew the answer. "My parents were Monarchists who hated Moroccans. Despite never having a sentimental connection to royal traditions myself, I have always been a strict Catholic. Friends of mine who advocated for Franco showed me snippets of what the Anarchists and Communists read. I did not like what Marx had to say about religion. I felt that I had to defend the Church."

Benno slurped the wine down as if it were a race. The drink dripped down the side of his mouth and fell off his chin as if he were spilling dark tears. Paco stood up to fetch another bottle from his cabinet. As he uncorked the bottle, he heard Erikah's voice from behind him.

"Do you feel you did right by your faith?"

"I will be forgiven, regardless," Paco said, as if he had rehearsed the response.

Paco turned around to see the couple staring at him. Humo was watching them, once again on guard as Paco's body tensed. He poured himself a glass before serving Benno. Benno continued with his retelling.

"Ernst served under Hugo just like his older brother. The Republicans shot him down over Madrid. Unlike Walter, our forces were not able to recover his body to properly lay him to rest."

Paco took out another cigarette when his went out. Benno's coat hung over the back of his chair, so Erikah reached into the pocket and pulled out the same lighter from before. She lit a cigarette for Paco and took one out of her own purse to smoke her own.

"You are a Catholic," Benno said. "You believe in the Holy Trinity. Our youngest boy, Otto, served in this last war."

"I believe I identified the pattern in this story," Paco said. "My condolences for your boys. All three of them."

They drank a while longer. Paco had stopped, now feeling the effects of intoxication. Benno's face sagged as his mouth dangled open and his eyes became incapable of focusing. Erikah, who had begun to drink conservatively, sat and smoked her cigarette between her sips. At one point she sat on the couch beside Humo. Humo protested, until Paco told him to cease. Erikah stroked his chin until Humo's tail began to wag.

"I am sorry to say, but I never met Ernst."

"He was a tall, handsome boy," Erikah said. "Brawny, too, with black hair, just like yours."

"I am sorry," Paco said. "Our paths never crossed."

Benno stood up and the chair legs scratched the wood as it slid back. He was inebriated and almost made him lose balance and collapse.

"The damn Hugo owes me three sons!" he shouted in Spanish. He continued to yell, but Paco could not translate his German, but recognized the word "wrath." Benno took a breath and looked over, appearing to gather his composure. "I need to relieve myself," he said, as he nearly stumbled outside.

Humo's tail still wagged, as Erikah stroked under his chin. "I might have been too hard on these people," the dog said. "Too quick to judge. I hardly ever do that."

"I apologize for my husband. We were just hoping to learn more about Ernst before we make our journey to South America," Erikah explained before pouring the wine down her throat. "We have no other family left alive. It is just us."

Paco walked over and sat beside her. Humo jumped off the couch and sat beside his feet.

"Do you believe wonderful things can be born from grief?" she asked.

"I believe that is where all wonderful things are born."

She put her hand on her stomach. "My grief is cradling life in my womb, right as we speak."

Paco was shocked. He thought she was too old to conceive. But he had been drinking, and was not rude enough to question the matter.

"It is still early," she said. "But I know it will be another boy. A son I will not let die fighting anyone else's war."

She finished her glass of wine. The color of the wine matched the dark shade of her red lipstick.

"You should check on Benno," she said. "He is very drunk and could wander away." She slunk into the cushions with a grin plastered across her face. "I am a lightweight," she admitted. "I feel woozy."

Erikah's eyes closed. Paco got up and began to walk to the door. But when he passed his trunk, Humo barked.

"Bring your gun!" he said. "Who knows what he's capable of."

"I thought you said you were too quick to judge them?"

"I don't remember saying that."

Paco opened his trunk and took the pistol resting on top of his old army uniform. Erikah was nearly asleep. She did not notice Paco hook the holster around his waist or hear him cock the pistol.

Paco went outside and saw that evening was approaching. Humo followed Paco and walked beside him in subordination. At the rear of his cottage, they found Benno sitting on a stool behind Alfonso.

"What are you doing out here?" Paco asked.

"Just admiring your steed," Benno slurred. He held his palms out towards Paco. "Der hoden," he said. "Enormous!"

"Look! Look! Look!" Humo yelled.

"What's gotten into you?" asked Paco.

"That damn bird is here!" he shouted.

Stationed on a nearby rock, they spotted the Egyptian Vulture with its orange beak and feathers that looked like needles on its neck.

"I told you I saw it!" Humo yelled.

Benno said something in German that Paco didn't understand. Benno took out his pistol and took aim at the bird to shoot.

"No! Wait!" Paco tried to warn.

Benno discharged the weapon. The echo from the blast boomed throughout the valley. His shot missed and the bird flew away as Humo continued to bark. The commotion frightened Alfonso, who bucked and kicked out his back hooves. The horseshoe collided against Benno's temple and Paco saw blood splatter. It was a horrific sight.

"Oh my God!" Humo shouted. "Did you see that?" He ran over to the body.

Paco crept towards Benno. There was no movement, and his head bled out onto the dirt as lay sprawled on his back.

Humo began sniffing the wound and the ground around him. "Disgusting. There's chunks of his brain around."

"Humo, get away."

"Yuck! It tastes awful."

"Why are you licking it?"

The commotion died down. Humo was no longer barking, Alfonso stopped bucking, and Benno had no more words to slur.

"You shot my husband."

Paco turned around and saw Erikah standing before them, with a pistol in her hand that he had not noticed before. From the sight of the scene, her accusation was not misplaced. But Paco was afraid he would not have the time to explain.

"Erikah, please," he said, reciting her name gently, in an attempt to sound familiar to her.

She took aim at Paco and pulled the trigger.

Humo yelled, "Guardián, look out!" before jumping in front of Paco.

Humo whimpered as he fell to the ground. Paco gasped in horror. Without thinking, Paco drew his weapon and fired. His lone shot hit Erikah in the forehead and she collapsed backwards.

"Great shot, Guardián," Humo said, now standing between the corpse and Paco.

"I thought she shot you!"

"No. I think she missed us both."

"Then why were you whimpering like she hit you?"

"It was so loud...I was scared."

Together, they both crept over towards the body. The scene terrified Paco, not able to believe what he had just done. Humo sniffed the corpse and the ground around her where the soil soaked up the blood.

"I can smell her brains on the ground," Humo said. "Yuck, they taste just like his!"

A couple hours passed, and no authorities came to the isolated area of the valley. Paco knew they were likely not going to arrive, but he wanted an opportunity to explain in case anyone who heard the gunfire decided to come and investigate. The land around him remained silent. The vultures and bugs would gather soon, and he did not want his home to resemble the battlefields he had seen during his years fighting.

He put on his army boots that he kept in the trunk, placed the couple in a wagon, and rolled them towards the thick patches of trees that made up miniature forests. As he rolled them through the dirt, he tried not to look down at their disfigured heads. The sight made him sick.

Surrounded by the trees, Paco began to dig with a gaslight lit beside him. He dug two holes beside each other near a tree offset from the others. The formation of the branches resembled a cross, which he felt was an appropriate marker for the grave site. He spent hours digging the two six-foot graves. When he finished, he hoisted the bodies up one at a time and dropped them in. With his eyes shut, and his head turned away, he positioned them with their arms crossed. Then he covered them with dirt. After the graves were filled, he recited a prayer. He kept it short and made the sign of the cross when he finished. Then he took the wagon and headed back to his cottage.

Paco parked the wagon beside Alfonso and walked past the drying blood on the ground. Humo was waiting by the door and jumped on Paco when he walked in. He wagged his rear, thrilled to see his friend again. Humo sniffed the dirt that covered Paco's boots. Benno's jacket still hung on the back of the chair. Dirty glasses and hollowed bottles of wine littered the cottage. The couple's duffel bag was by the door. Paco assumed it contained all their possessions from Berlin. Paco slipped off his boots and collapsed onto the couch. Humo sat beside him; upright as if he was imitating a human.

"She was pregnant," Paco muttered. "I murdered a pregnant woman."

"They are the ones that came in here and caused trouble. I never trusted either of them, anyway," Humo said.

"They came to learn more about their son and now they're dead. All because of me."

"Don't feel too bad for them. The man couldn't even kill that vile vulture!" Humo yelled.

Paco took a cigarette out of his pocket. His hands trembled as he slipped a smoke out of the pack. He saw the couple's lighter with the swastika symbol engraved.

Paco thought about all the newspapers he read during the last war. The headlines called attention to death, destruction, and genocide. He focused on those words and recited them in his head, which had a calming effect that allowed him to control his breathing.

"They owned a factory," Paco said. "And she was pregnant. I killed a pregnant woman. I never killed a pregnant woman before."

"Well, that you know of," Humo said. "God only knows the people that got killed by those bombs you dropped."

Humo spoke with such innocence, as if he meant his comment to bring comfort. The words Paco heard only made him cry. He wept until the skin on his face and palms became damp. When he lifted his palms from his face, Humo would lean forward to sniff the tears before he licked them.

It was now dark, and Humo looked out the window as if he had just noticed.

"If you want my opinion," the dog said. "I think this was a peculiar day."

Paco let out an abrupt, solitary laugh, and saliva fell from his mouth and landed on his knee. Humo collapsed into his guardian's lap and Paco massaged his ear.

"Today, you saw first hand that I am a wicked man," Paco said. "I always said that God will forgive me, but I don't know. How could he? Why should he?"

"That does not make sense, Guardián," Humo said with earnest, while still resting on Paco's lap. "I love you. So how could you be a bad person? It's illogical."

Despite the depression, Paco smiled, even though his stomach was in knots and the heaviness paralyzed him. He still had Humo, and as he pet the dog he noted that his curly hair reminded him of springboards. It was so quiet through the cottage that the only noise Paco could hear was heavy breathing. Humo stretched and let out a grunt, then he rolled over on his back and let out a deep sigh.

"Rub my belly, please," he requested. Paco obliged.

Cornerstone

CAREN MESSING

"I'll rummage—you sift," Harvey says.

My brother places both hands on my shoulders and ushers me to the side. Then, waving his arms in a grand sweep, he spins one hundred eighty degrees to face our grandfather's "Closet That Ate Manhattan."

Harvey slams open a rusted stepladder, and stares motionless at the closet, with arms akimbo as I stand by his side, numb. He launches the stepladder with ritual reluctance and approaches the precipice. Teetering on the top rung, he catches his balance, flexes his knees and hips and dives his upper body into the closet. Rooting through an inextricable abyss of ninety years of accretion has begun.

Harvey's vociferous rummaging assaults my nervous system. It sounds like an entire drum-kit falling down a steep staircase. From the top shelf, Harvey pulls out the first box and lets it fall to the floor *thm*. It makes the sound of a bass drum stuffed with a pillow.

I maneuver the box away from the hazard zone of Harvey's stepladder. I empty the contents of the box onto the floor in front of me and scan the pile of different things like a helicopter surveying the topography of a strange land. There's a slow-motion galaxy of dust suspended in the shaft of sun-spilling-light cascading through the window. How many hours did my grandfather gaze on this same shaft of light as he smoked his pipe in this apartment? I kneel, my knees creaking like the old wooden-plank floor itself.

Now to 'sift.' I hover over the pile of varied personal effects and get lost in the medley of alternating shadow and sun-streaked corrugations from the Venetian-blind window-treatment. *Hmmm...let's see here...Here are a couple of loose keys,* I muse. Their steel, jagged edges are like serrated smiles glinting in the evanescent glee of rediscovery. A Rock and Roll comeback amid years of neglect and disuse.

Behind me I hear an arrhythmic *teh-teh teh-teh* sound like a drum kit with minimal decay. Harvey is having a wrestling match with a time-worn, two-wheeled folding cart that's wedged in the closet. A clothes hanger is inter *teh-teh* twined in the metal rods of the cart and the integrated hook used to hang onto a supermarket shopping-cart.

I focus on the panoply of items and pick up a small, circular tin box containing buttons and a penny or two. Lifting one penny up to the blazing sunlight, I squint and move it as though playing a trombone.

What year is on this penny? Might it be a rare 1943 copper penny? If so it would be worth a lot of money, I thought.

I remember one day my grandfather said, "Did you know that during wartime, in 1943, the U.S. Mint stopped production of copper pennies? You see, copper was in high demand to make shell casings for WWII and the treasury made steel pennies dipped in zinc oxide instead. You know what that is, right?"

Hmmm... I wonder if this penny is one of the few error coins accidentally struck on a copper planchet in the U.S. Mint. I hold it up in the sunlight again. *Nope.* The year on the penny reads "1969."

The coin is worth only a mere cent... A-mere-cent-worth. ("Amir Scentworth"—what a swell guy!) Just a cent. "1969," eh? Just a scent of free love, man! A connection. Boy, if this penny could talk...

I look over my shoulder at Harvey, but he has disappeared except for his butt sticking out from the closet.

I yell, "Heads or Tails?!?" then flip the penny up, catch it, smack it down on the backside of my opposite hand and, then, cover it. After hearing no response, I announced "I call Tails!" I lift my palm slowly and uncover it: "Tails it is!."

I toss the coin back in the tin box. It lands with a barely perceptible *plip* sound. Closing the box and shaking it, I imagine it's a percussive maraca and *shake-shake shake-shake.*

"I said *'sift'* not *'shake'*" Harvey emerges from the threshold of the closet with an expression of bewildered exasperation. It was the same expression he had when I told him I wanted to be a ventriloquist when I grew up.

As if exhaling a long drag of a cigarette while conducting an imaginary orchestra, he says, "Sifft." Simultaneously, he glides his hands laterally through space indicating a slow, undulating ocean. I imagine him dancing the hula while wearing a grass skirt and a pink orchid behind his ear under a full moon in Hawaii.

He resumes his rummaging and yanks an old ironing board out of the closet. He bashes it atop the two-wheel metal cart making intermittent metallic *psh* sounds like reverberating drum cymbals. Then, two dilapidated leather suitcases come tumbling down upon each other with a *bmm-diddle-dmmm* tom-tom drum sound. One of the crumbling suitcases springs open, and our grandfather's stamp collection binder pops out.

My brother starts coughing, probably from the dust, and when we lock eyes, mid-cough he points to my pile and manages the "gliding-water gesture" again. I am simultaneously impressed and annoyed with his capacity to delegate while he is choking for air.

I salute him, "Yes sir! Got it: you rummage, I sift. Roger that. Okay, okay..."

Now in a coughing fit, Harvey leaves the room and slams the door behind him. He gropes to the kitchen for something to drink. The pitch-sound of his coughing drops lower and lower in a Doppler effect.

I hear running water from the kitchen faucet. Then, I hear the kitchen cabinets *open-slam, open-slam, and open-slam.*

Harvey yells, "Well, it looks like Papa has the set of China and crystalware after all... Ugh! Getting the kitchen together is going to take forever—and forever I don't have—especially when I need to meet Elise by 5:00 PM."

I refocus, placing the tin box aside. *Hmmmmm, there's a busted, cork-screwing nylon guitar string—this can be thrown out.* I place it in the reject pile. *A Swingline stapler—wow, that's an oldie... I bet I could use this.* I place it in the keep pile. *Oh cool, a magnifying glass!*

Then I open a flat, gray metal container and peer in to find one of the many reels of our grandfather's 16mm film. I wonder if this is an archive of some home movies. *Maybe footage of our father as a child? Maybe of our parents' wedding?* The film resides in its circular canister like a model of continuity we can perpetually project but not experience.

I take the magnifying glass and metal canister of 16mm film into the kitchen. Harvey looks at me. He raises his wrist and taps it twice, gesturing that we are running against the clock. I hand salute him which immediately turns into a make believe karate chop dance, and I vocalize play fighting sound effects I haven't imitated since we were kids.

I move closer to the kitchen window which is partially obstructed by two dish towels. They hang stiffly on a three armed wall-mounted metal towel bar. The towels are faded in color and as I remove them from the towel bar, they're so stiff that when I place them on the counter, they maintain a spine in the area where they were folded. My hands cannot flatten or smooth them despite my attempts. I didn't realize how sweaty my palms were until now.

I take the 16mm film out of the canister and lay the strip against one of the metal towel bars. Then I stagger the position of one of the other metal arms to span the film along these supports. The light spills into the room from the adjacent window and illuminates the frames in the film.

I peer through the magnifying glass at the still frames of a spatial world. The sprocket holes demarcate such evenly spaced events in contours bright and dark. I see people with newspaper hats and umbrellas in the rain. I see some faces in a window, "Is this the way out?" their faces seem to say. *Who are these people? Did my grandfather help them leave during the war? Is this Poland?* I move the strip of film along. I see a young woman's face rising from a pillow. *Wow—is this my grandmother?* Yes, with her big, almond shaped eyes and full lips. It looks like she was sleeping, she was lying on her side with her body partially concealed beneath blankets. *Is this after they had sex?* Then I see her hand blindly grazing a ticking clock in the blue shadows of dawn: the clock reads half past six o'clock. She is disentangling from the blankets and laughing.

I carefully return the film into the canister. I'll definitely research a company that can transfer 16mm to a digital format. It'll be pricey but maybe Harvey will split the cost. I go back to the living room, place the canister in the keep pile and resume sifting.

I pick up a three inch metal item which looks, at first, like a nail clipper. It has three interlocked, though, separate pieces that can be unfolded like a pocket knife. Upon further inspection I realize that it's our grandfather's metal pipe kit with tamper, pick, and reamer. I used to play with this, pretending it was a bird: I'd stand it up on the tamper, position the pick at ninety degrees dorsally (as though tail feathers) and position the reamer at one hundred thirty-five degrees ventrally (as though a bird face with beak).

I see a scatter of paper clips and a letter opener. *Hmmm, this letter opener has the same decorative handle as the magnifying glass—they must be part of the same desk set.* I put it in the keep pile.

Here's an old silver and black Timex wristwatch with a "Twist-O-Flex" band. I remember the television commercials about Timex watches—"It takes a licking and keeps on ticking." The watch face reads a quarter past three o'clock. I shake the watch a few times and place it to my ear—no tick or tock. I imagine my grandfather holding it to his ear too. Like we are both leaning in, listening to a seashell for a barely audible sound of the ocean. I put the watch around my left wrist.

I see lost pieces to different jigsaw puzzles. One puzzle piece is the color of green seaweed. Another puzzle piece has an image of a slate-blue eye. There are some conjoined puzzle pieces—a partial image of an ear with sideburns that continue downward like mutton chops.

Suddenly, I see my grandfather seated at an olive-colored portable bridge table in his bungalow in the Catskills. I remember the hours and hours with him at the table doing one puzzle after the next.

"First things first," he'd say. Then, he'd take a long draw from his pipe. He withdrew it from his mouth and tilted his chin upwardly. His mouth took the embouchure for creating countless smoke-rings: they undulated and dissipated in mesmerizing shapes, like vortices of ancient hieroglyphs.

"First: find the outermost pieces—especially the corners!" He gestured with a pipe in his hand as he spoke. He was a man of few words but he mentored with a patience unknown.

As my fingers comb the spread of items, I pick up another puzzle piece: it has a sienna and yellow hue. The piece is notable due to its curved exterior edge. I feel my entire body melt into the realization that this must be from that *circular* puzzle. My grandfather and I did this one puzzle that was dizzying. It was a fifteen hundred piece circular puzzle with an empty space in the center. The center hole in the puzzle was probably four inches in diameter.

"Think of this puzzle like the shape of your favorite doughnut, with a hollow center," my grandfather said.

Now, if it had been a puzzle of a French Cruller (my favorite hollow, twisted cake) I might have enjoyed the torus-shaped journey, but this puzzle was no piece of cake—rather it was a "Kalachakra Esoteric Mandala Puzzle." My grandfather said that in Buddhism, "Kalachakra" meant wheel of time or "time-cycles." The puzzle's mandalic image balanced abstract, opposite shapes around a shared point. Yet, this "shared point" was an empty space. The point was a hole. So my grandfather's strategy to "find the outermost pieces first" didn't help. *Was it an outermost piece or an innermost piece?* Some pieces had a continuous, convexly curved edge whereas others had a continuous, concavely curved edge; they could either be the "outermost" pieces or could be the "innermost" pieces. *Was it still an exterior edge or an interior one?* I searched for the puzzle pieces that might frame the elusive center first, but how was I supposed to "frame" something with no corners!? I felt lost in a labyrinthine quest as all certainty in my approach was overturned.

"Be patient," he said. "You're not supposed to know. You'll find out when you get there."

A centripetal journey to find hidden centers. How could we not have slipped under its spell—*it was fading or was it deepening?*

When we finally completed the puzzle my grandfather leaned back in his bridge chair, but I felt oddly unsatisfied. I noticed that the empty space in the center of the puzzle framed an imperfection in the olive tabletop marked by masking tape, which had been used to bandage a rip in the vinyl covering. The puzzle remained on the tabletop for the rest of the summer.

Soon after, an unspoken ritual evolved: we took turns placing things in the center. Usually, I'd feature a different member of my rubber monster collection while he chose to display a different smoking pipe. One day, I would position my rubber monster King-Kong with his mouth agape and one arm flexed in conquest in the middle of the puzzle (I propped him up against a tin Band-Aid box). On another day, my grandfather's half-bent Billiard pipe with the yellow shank would be on display. Another time, my floppy, orange rubber lobster from our trip to the New York Aquarium in Coney Island, Brooklyn. Then, his brown Calabash pipe, which I loved, since it was so Sherlock Holmes-like. Once, I surprised him and crafted a wiry-fuzzy butterfly made from his multi-colored pipe-cleaners.

Sometimes, the new centerpiece stayed for days. At other times, only a few hours—but one thing was certain, it would not be until I deliberately removed my monster of choice that he would, then, place his chosen pipe. We could each inhabit the center as long as we liked and not until we each removed our *own* displayed items would the other, then, grace the center.

The center, which revealed that imperfect, jagged vinyl covered with masking tape, was an open secret and led to something safe: a mutually revered and consecrated space. A celebration. We'd catch up to something that had already happened—mutually sharing (eye brows raised) an exquisite conversation in which we never uttered a word.

On my eleventh birthday the air was cool like spearmint. The sky's apricot colored sun-setting rays cascaded the expanse of the lake. I entered the bungalow to find a birthday cake in the center of the puzzle. The flickering candle flames glistened so the shapes on the mandala puzzle undulated and stretched like a shadow dancing to a vanishing point. I blew out the candles.

"May this be the best year for all of us," he said with eyelids wrinkling.

As we sat together, amid the vaporous ascension of the candles' smoke trails, the sounds of tree frogs, crickets, and cicadas seem to crescendo in a resounding euphony.

Suddenly, Harvey calls out to me from the other room. "Are you sifting?!? We are running out of time!" The abruptness of his voice spikes between my ears *clap* like a clapperboard cueing sound during filmmaking.

"Yes, Yes," I mutter, dismissively, flicking my wrist like the tail of a horse swatting flies from its rear end.

I glance at my wrist, my grandfather's silver and black Timex watch still says a quarter past three o'clock. How many years has it been a quarter past three o'clock? The second hand stripped of momentum—-no longer offering evenly spaced events, here and now there. Without motion there's no animation of the spatial world—it is like a single frame or screenshot of a film: here and nowhere else.

I wonder what my grandfather was doing or feeling when it stopped? Maybe we were together. Can time run out? Well, if his watch can't tell me what time it is—perhaps it can teach me *what* "time" is.

Be patient and sift. I graze the puzzle-piece edges which feel like my grandfather's skin—like cigarette paper. His wrists were like little branches, when he sifted through puzzle pieces his fingers fluttered like a bird flying away.

We are still hovering and sifting together. Hover and sift. Hover and sift.

The silence comes sculptured by spoken dreams, like sudden light filling a room—an infinite approach sifting in silence in the plenitude of the "present."

°

Escaping the Party

C.W. BIGELOW

I crawled out of Marsha's bedroom closet, struggling to lift the window noiselessly, before hoisting myself up and sitting hunched on the windowsill staring down at the story and a half plunge through nightfall. There was no luxury of choice or ability to calculate the landing. I understood the risk of an awkward touchdown; a jolt that could shove my legs right into my pelvis, a loud double-snap echoing gruesomely in my imagination, along with the realization it would reduce my height of which I had no surplus—or crack one or both tibias—the bones piercing right through my skin like a stiletto or break both my arms if I was forced to use them to break the fall; which would certainly mean walking around for months in casts. It did cross my mind how cool it would be to have all my friends sign them—tantamount to having ink covering my limbs, without of course, having to make it permanent. That was if I could keep my face from crashing into the ground in such a precarious angle my neck would shatter, which might leave me paralyzed or end up being the last act of my life, which meant all the aforementioned risks would be moot.

From behind the line of Marsha's clothes—hanger after hanger of neatly hung shirts, pants, and dresses awash in the sweet rose scent of her perfume, I watched through the slit in the door, a squat, bald officer walk to the window and attempt to open it.

"It's locked, so no one has escaped through here."

His partner, a tall thin man still wearing his hat, whispered, "I hear something in the hallway."

"

I swallowed hard and bit my tongue. He must have heard the pounding of my heart careening around the closet, spilling out into the hall.

I wondered why the two of them seemed so hellbent. Was it some sort of calling? Did they see themselves as teachers or were they just power mongers flexing their muscles in hopes of scaring the shit out of us and taking great pleasure in handing out punishment. Maybe they were just doing their job, or maybe they were irritated at being called away from dinner where they had been involved in a deep conversation about kids of their own.

The squeak of a door down the hall gave me my signal and I jumped into her bedroom. If her proposal came to fruition we would be in her double bed under the pink flowered bedspread, between matching pink flowered lamp shades under a concert poster—black and white, but indistinguishable from my current vantage point. That potent rose-scented perfume filled the air. It tickled my nose and I had to swallow a sneeze, which would have meant my capture.

Considering their reasons, I began questioning my own motives, and the payback I was risking. Selfish is as selfish does, and I was wrapped in a blanket of guilt as I balanced on the windowsill. I hoped I could learn something from this exercise, this escape, if in fact I could escape. Learning without punishment—a novel concept.

"If you come to my party you can spend the night," Marsha said before our yearbook meeting in the journalism trailer behind the high school.

I nodded, not paying much attention. Our only connection was our work on the yearbook staff, which meant meetings after class. She was a year younger and collected and organized the pictures from our staff photographer, Billy. I was the sports editor. Since she had no experience on an athletic team, I was confused why she volunteered to help me, since I did not have much of a team, I gladly accepted her offer.

Twenty-degree frigidity slapped me in the face reminding me of the urgency of the situation. Flexing my legs like I was on a diving platform, trying to envision the dark, frozen lawn as a deep swimming pool, which could reduce the harm. Extend my arms, or keep them tucked in to prevent them from breaking the fall, which might in fact snap them into pieces, but then, what could I use for balance while dropping that far?

Marsha greeted me at the door with a kiss, and I smelled the strong odor of beer on her breath and tasted the pungency on her tongue as she shoved it into my mouth. "I'm so happy you came." She was slurring a bit. "You're staying the whole night, aren't you?"

"If you want."

She reached up and kissed me again, pulling me close and grabbing my ass. "What does this tell you?"

I smiled and nodded. The house was full of her friends, some walking by with beers in their hands, others filling up couches, chairs, and space. The music was so loud it was hard to hear her voice.

Billy handed me a beer as he passed us. Marsha took my hand, led me to a closet where I hung my coat, then down a set of stairs into a sunken living room. Billy found a spot on the couch with Brenda, toasting me with a smirk as if Brenda, who was Marsha's best friend, had let him in on the plan. The people moving slowly through the room were Marsha's crowd. They stared at me, which made me feel naked. Billy was the only one I knew. The rest were faces from school hallways and classes.

I had been dropped off by a friend, purposely arriving late, in order to give Marsha a chance to decide if she wanted to go through with her plan, and not having to worry about getting my parents' car back that night. The commotion from the brightly lit house was palpable as I approached. The street was crowded with parked cars.

Billy's expression changed from a smirk to alarm—his eyes growing to pancakes, focusing passed my shoulder. I turned to see two uniformed cops crowding the doorway.

As one of the girls called for Marsha, I dropped her hand and bounded up the stairs to the third floor of the house. Her bedroom was the first door on the left, and I ducked into the closet.

The reason for my cowardice was my previous run-ins with the law. My parents had finally forgiven me for putting them through multiple embarrassing incidents and another one so soon was certainly not what any of us needed.

Did I have empathy for Marsha? Absolutely. I'd been in her situation before. Luckily, I was aware enough to ask for a warrant, which they could not produce, and I promised them I would quiet the place down so my neighbors could finally sleep. It seemed to be enough for those cops, unfortunately, the cops at her door weren't as forgiving.

Still hoping to somehow complete our mission, I soared off the windowsill, through the black, frosty night, arms spread like an eagle to keep my balance, preparing to curl and roll as I crashed onto the grass—which arrived much faster than expected—harder, crunchier, and icier than I was ready for—knocking the wind out of me. Painfully gasping for air, I rolled over and bounded into a sprint—reminiscent of my hundred yard dashes—exploding out of the starter blocks at the sound of the gun. I hoped for silence, no gunshots ringing in the night air as I dashed through the backyards before sneaking around the block to walk along the cross street to her cul-de-sac. Relieved but disappointed, figuring the escape was an even exchange for the lost opportunity. The cop car blocked the mouth of the cul-de-sac to make sure there would be no car escapes.

The steam billowing from my mouth reminded me that my coat was still in the closet and it would be a long, cold walk home—even worse I realized my phone was still in that coat. It was an hour of looking back over my shoulder in fear, worrying the duo of cops would pull up behind me before I finally reached home.

I greeted my parents in the living room, which meant going back was out of the question.

"I thought you were staying out tonight."

I caught a hint of disappointment in my mom's voice. I guess we were both on the losing end of the night. "I decided to come home." No reason. It wasn't a lie because if the cops had vacated, I would have gone back. Without a coat it was impossible to survive a long wait. At least the long walk kept me warmer.

She asked no further questions and I retired to my bedroom where I called Marsha. It rang four times until her father's recorded voice sounded on the answering machine. I decided it best to not try and contact her the rest of the weekend, figuring her parents would be filling her time.

"Here's your coat," Billy said as he plopped it on the table in the journalism trailer Monday morning.

"Thanks, I was hoping it would be discovered before her parents found it."

"I had mine in my car, so I grabbed it on my way out."

"Good." I grabbed my phone out of the inside pocket and plugged it into the charger.

"I followed you up the stairs as soon as I could. I saw that open window and didn't hesitate," he explained. "I stuck my head out, ready to pitch my body into the night, figuring I could catch up with you. I was lucky I had to slow down to get through the window because as soon as I looked down, that tall cop said, 'Wouldn't be jumping, buddy boy, unless you want to eat a bullet.' He was waiting with his Glock aimed up at me."

"The long exodus of party goers began at that point. Parents were called under the guidance of those two cops," he continued as he unloaded his camera equipment onto a table in the trailer. "Feeling guilty about his excessive force, he let me off."

"That's good news," I said. The door behind me creaked open.

"They never could get ahold of my parents," Marsha said as she walked over. "See you got your coat."

Her tone was mocking as she passed me and sat down next to Billy.

"Yea," he chuckled, "but we had to explain it to them when they got home yesterday." He avoided making eye contact with me as he attached a wide-angle lens onto his camera and placed it back into his bag.

A wide smile crept across Marsha's blushing face as she reached over and took Billy's hand and looked into his eyes. "They were impressed by your courage and manners, Billy."

He shrugged as he packed his camera in his bag and waited for her to stand up. She took his hand. They said nothing more, leaving me with the echoes of their footsteps. I smirked as I recalled the cavalcade of emotions I wrestled with all weekend. Sometimes things do work out for the best.

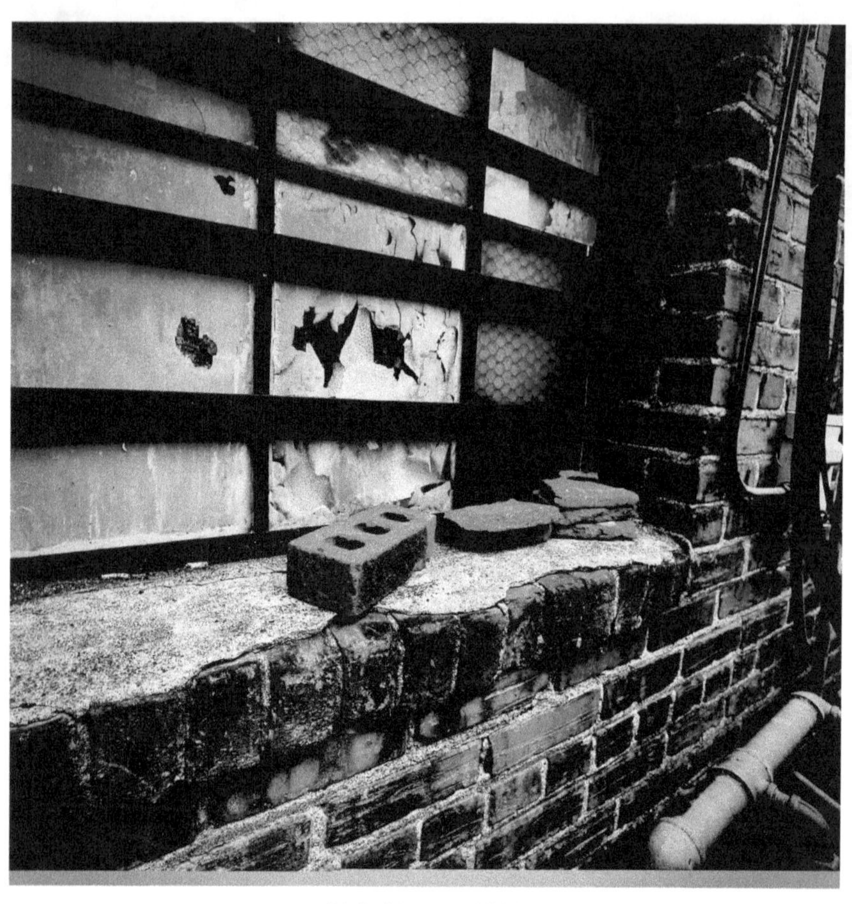

Digital Image, 2020
william c. crawford

Floyd and the Magic Spectacles

WAYNE BOWEN

"So then, Floyd, what do we call the side opposite the ninety-degree angle in a right triangle?" Mrs. Wilson asked, with a hopeful ring to her voice.

Floyd had yet to answer a question correctly in her class, but she refused to give up on him; partly because she genuinely wanted to see him succeed, and partly because she felt that the failure of any of her students was a direct reflection of her ability as a teacher. Floyd sat staring at her with a completely blank expression on his thin face. He licked his lips nervously, flashed his usual helpless smile, and finally shrugged his skinny shoulders. At this, Cedric, a big and muscular boy, who sat directly behind Floyd, snickered then slapped the palm of his hand on his desktop as if to show his amusement.

At last, Shamika, the best student in Mrs. Wilson's fourth period geometry class, blurted out, "Why are you trying to embarrass him, Mrs. Wilson? You know he doesn't have a clue what the answer is."

Mrs. Wilson was taken aback. She did not know how to respond to this unexpected accusation. Then she took a deep breath and replied, "Shamika, in my class I expect every student to learn. No exceptions."

Just then the bell rang and the students quickly gathered their materials and headed out the door. As Cedric passed Floyd's desk, he bent over and whispered, "What a fucking dumbass you are!"

Floyd's body jerked, and his chin slowly sank down onto his chest. With an air of profound resignation, he crammed his things into his backpack, stood up, and ambled over to Mrs. Wilson's desk, at which she was now seated with the stunned expression still lingering on her visage. Floyd stopped and uttered in a sad little voice, "I'm so sorry, ma'am. I just can't get it."

She straightened up, smoothed her skirt, and said in her most business-like tone, "I want you to come in tomorrow morning for some extra help, say about 8:30 AM. Can you do that?"

Eyes focused on his dirty sneakers, Floyd stood silently for a couple of seconds, then shook his head and stated in a clear, quiet voice, "It won't do no good, ma'am. I'm just too dumb."

Before Mrs. Wilson could recover from her second shock of the morning, Floyd had shuffled out the door and disappeared down the hallway.

Later that afternoon, as Floyd trudged across a vacant lot on his way home, kicking a stone along in front of him, his thoughts kept reverting to his humiliating failure that day in Mrs. Wilson's class.

How come I don't ever know the right answer? he asked himself disconsolately. *She keeps goin' over the same stuff, and I can't seem to remember nothin,'* he thought.

Floyd's geometry textbook was bouncing along in his backpack, and he knew that, as he did every evening before a school day, he would spend the evening trying to make heads or tails of his homework, but to no avail. It was not just math he had problems with, either. He was barely passing English, biology, and all the rest of his classes.

Maybe I just need to drop out of school and get a job, he mused—or *maybe just run away.*

Floyd had once seen an old movie on tv where a poor boy ran away from home and got a job on a sailing ship. He had had a lot of exciting adventures among the South Sea Islands, and after many years, ended up a rich sea captain. At the end of the movie, he returned home to astonish his elderly parents—who had believed their son lost forever. Floyd could imagine the look on his own mother's face when he returned home after many years—a fabulously wealthy businessman with his own private jet, a fleet of limousines, and a yacht in every port in the world. She would be so proud of him. Then he remembered the disappointment on her face when she had seen his last report card. Floyd kicked the stone as hard as he could, and muttered to himself, "I'll never amount to nothin'."

Then Floyd noticed something shiny on the ground near the place where the stone had landed. His youthful curiosity piqued and he hurried forward to see what it was. There on the ground lay a pair of black plastic-framed men's eyeglasses. He quickly picked them up for a closer examination. One of the lenses was cracked and both ear pieces were caked with dried mud. He scraped off the mud with a thumbnail and placed the glasses on his face. The whole world immediately became blurry, and as he moved his head back and forth, everything he saw wobbled and shifted about fantastically. He suddenly felt dizzy, pulled the glasses off, turned them this way and that way in his hand to look at them from every angle, and then, he pressed his thumb against the good lenses until they popped out. After placing the front of the glasses flat against the ground, he picked up a twig that was lying nearby, and punched out the cracked lenses with a couple of swift thrusts. Then he stuffed the empty frames in his backpack and headed for home.

After dinner that evening, Floyd retired to his bedroom to engage in his usual struggle with his homework. He opened his geometry textbook and sat staring at the page entitled, "Properties of Right Triangles" for a couple of minutes. Then he sighed deeply, plopped his elbows down on the desktop, and sat for several more minutes with his head cradled forlornly between his hands. Suddenly his face brightened—he stood up, rummaged around in his backpack for a moment, and then pulled out the black plastic frames. He placed them on his face and turned to look at himself in his dresser mirror. He was amazed at what he saw. Instead of thin-faced, stupid-looking Floyd, he was confronted with a complete stranger, a young man of obvious intelligence and competence, a young man who could make short work of right triangles, Civil War battles, and photosynthesis. He removed the frames, and there he was again—dumb old Floyd. He put the frames back on and smiled at his impressive reflection in the mirror.

Floyd sat down at his desk and started to read. At first, just like usual, nothing made any sense to him; but the "new" Floyd was not to be deterred. While reading over the explanation of the Pythagorean Theorem for the third time, he suddenly looked up with a wide-eyed expression of surprise.

"I got it!" Floyd exclaimed. He reread the explanation, laughed aloud, and said, "It's real easy. The square of the hypotenuse of a right triangle is equal to the sum of the squares of the other two sides. Why did I find that so hard before?"

He removed the frames from his face and examined them. No matter which way he turned them, he could detect nothing in their construction or on the smooth plastic surface that provided any indication of the power they seemed to possess. He put them back on, took a sheet of paper out of his binder, and started on his next homework assignment.

Floyd had an idea—he knew the answers to the odd-numbered problems were in the back of the book, why not do them to see if he really understood? He worked problem one then flipped to the back of the book to check his answer. *Bingo!* It was right. A broad smile spread across his face. Floyd worked the rest of the odd-numbered problems, checking each one after he finished to confirm he had it right. At last, he sat back and stared at his finished assignment—there were only right answers on the page. He felt an amazing sense of confidence diffuse itself throughout his entire being; a sense that he had never experienced before. Floyd eagerly worked the even-numbered problems, and then put his pencil down and stared at his completed geometry homework with a tremendous feeling of satisfaction. *When Mrs. Wilson sees this, she's gonna freak out*, he thought to himself.

The next morning Floyd arrived at his first period English classroom before any of his classmates. He was sitting at his desk reviewing the assigned chapter from *A Tale of Two Cities* when Shamika walked in. She stopped and stared at Floyd for a few moments.

"When did you start wearing glasses?" she inquired testily.

Floyd grinned at her and replied, "Yesterday evening."

Shamika came closer, bent over, and took a long look at the black-rimmed spectacles—she frowned, straightened up, and said in an exasperated voice, "they don't even have any lenses. How are they gonna make you see better?"

Floyd's smile widened and he quickly glanced around the room to assure himself that no one else had come in.

"They're not for my eyes. They're for my brain." he whispered. Then he winked at her, leaned back in his desk, and resumed his review.

Shamika's jaw dropped. She glared at him and then slammed her bookbag down on her desk, shook her head.

"You've done some stupid things, Floyd, but this is the stupidest of all," she yelled.

Before Floyd could retort, Mr. Cahill, the English teacher, entered the classroom.

"Good morning, Shamika." He said as he placed his briefcase on his desk. As Mr. Cahill started to open his briefcase, he noticed Floyd, and paused with the lid halfway open.

"Uh, is that, uh, you, Floyd?" he finally managed to stammer.

Floyd nodded with a broad grin on his face.

Later, during the first class period, Mr. Cahill asked his students, "What is the significance of the scene with the broken wine cask outside Defarge's wine shop?"

Both Shamika and Floyd raised their hands.

Assuming Floyd did not know the answer, Mr. Cahill called on Shamika, who replied,

"Dickens is showing us that the citizens of Paris are so poor and hungry that they will even scoop up wine from the dirty streets."

Mr. Cahill nodded approvingly and said, "Very good, Shamika."

Then he noticed Floyd was still waving his arm insistently. *He probably just needs to go to the bathroom*, Mr. Cahill thought to himself.

Mr. Cahill sighed and asked, "Yes, Floyd, what is it?"

Floyd pushed his black frames up onto the bridge of his nose and responded.

"I think the red wine is like the blood that will be spilled during the revolution you told us about." Floyd's classmates gasped.

Mr. Cahill's lips began to move as if he were trying to say something, but not a sound came out for several seconds. At last he muttered incoherently, "You think, uh...I mean...well, uh..." After an awkward silence, he cleared his throat and said in a small voice, "That's exactly right, Floyd."

Floyd beamed at his classmates. Shamika stared at him in astonishment.

Soon word spread among the students about Floyd's remarkable metamorphosis. When Cedric heard from a couple of classmates that Floyd had correctly answered questions in English and biology, and that his black-framed glasses made him look smart, he was skeptical.

"That stupid jerk wouldn't know a right answer if it bit him on the ass," he growled. "I'm tellin' ya, it's just a put-up job between him and the teachers."

Cedric found himself looking forward to fourth period, the only class he had with Floyd. He could hardly wait to see this so-called "transformation" for himself, especially since he struggled in geometry almost as much as Floyd did. Cedric knew that if by some miracle Floyd really had gotten smarter, then he would be the dumbest student in class—a prospect he did not relish.

When the bell rang, signaling the end of third period, Cedric grabbed his backpack, raced to Mrs. Wilson's classroom, planted himself in his seat and stared impatiently at the door. Floyd sauntered in with a smirk on his bespectacled face and walked to his desk right, which was directly in front of Cedric's.

Then Floyd said, "Good morning, my good man" in a patronizing tone.

Cedric's brow furrowed and he snarled, "Fuck you, asshole!"

Floyd smiled benignly and sat down. Cedric was baffled. Not only did the black plastic frames make Floyd look intellectual, but they also seemed to endow him with a boldness he had never exhibited before.

Cedric punched Floyd on the shoulder and demanded, "Let me see them glasses!"

Floyd winced, but then turned halfway around and retorted, "No way!"

Cedric was stunned. He seized Floyd's collar in a muscular grip and was about to rip the frames from his face, when Mrs. Wilson walked in. Cedric let go and growled to himself between clenched teeth as he settled back in his desk.

"Wait till this afternoon,motherfucker!"

When Mrs. Wilson noticed Floyd's spectacles, she stared at him for a few moments perplexed and then exclaimed, "Good heavens, Floyd! I didn't know that you needed glasses."

Floyd smiled broadly and responded, "I started wearing them yesterday, ma'am."

Mrs. Wilson began instruction by checking to see if the students had understood the homework. She thought it best to start on a positive note and directed her first question to Shamika, her star student.

"Shamika, what is the Pythagorean Theorem?" Mrs. Wilson asked. She was surprised, however, to see Floyd's hand shoot up immediately.

Shamika beamed as she promptly and correctly answered the question.

Next Mrs. Wilson turned to Cedric and asked in a less confident tone, "Cedric, what is the equation for the Pythagorean Theorem?"

Again, Floyd's hand shot up.

Cedric sat silently with downcast eyes then he cleared his throat and muttered, "Uh, I dunno, ma'am."

Floyd, who had been waving his arm frantically, could contain himself no longer.

"It's $a^2 + b^2 = c^2$, ma'am," he blurted out.

Cedric felt his face get hot. He had just been upstaged by the biggest moron in the school.

At first Mrs. Wilson was dumbfounded. All she could do was stare at the bespectacled stranger who was sitting there beaming at her as broadly as Shamika had done before.

Finally, she stammered, "Uh, well, yes, Floyd...that's, uh, exactly right."

Floyd grinned at Shamika, who was gazing at Floyd as if he were a square egg, then turned and said to Cedric, "I'll be glad to tutor you if you need help."

Cedric's blood boiled. He gripped the desktop with all his strength to keep himself from springing on Floyd and pounding him to a bloody pulp.

Frightened by the fierce scowl that had suddenly appeared on Cedric's face, Mrs. Wilson hastily announced, "Well then, let's go on with the lesson."

That afternoon as Floyd was crossing the vacant lot on his way home, he heard voices behind him. He turned his head and saw Cedric and a couple of his roughneck friends walking directly towards him at a brisk pace. Floyd's heart leapt into his throat and he started to run, but his heavy backpack slowed him down. Before he knew it, Cedric had cut off his retreat and was standing right in front of him—his face a twisted mask of rage.

"Where the hell you think you're goin', asshole?" Cedric demanded.

Floyd glanced side-to-side and saw to his despair that Cedric's pals were blocking all avenues of escape. Floyd swallowed hard, choking down the panic that was rising within him, he lifted his hand to push the spectacles, which had slipped while he was running, back up on his nose. Then, to his astonishment, an unexpected feeling of reckless defiance began to dissolve the fear that had threatened to overwhelm him. He took a deep breath, smirked at Cedric, and asked in the most sarcastic tone he could muster, "Ready for your first tutoring session?"

Cedric's reaction was so swift that Floyd had no chance to dodge the powerful blow that caught him on the cheekbone, sending the frames flying off his face. Floyd fell down in a heap and lay there stunned for several seconds. Floyd rolled onto his knees, and as he raised one leg to try to stand up, he heard Cedric say in a high-pitched, sing-song voice, "Look at me, everyone. I'm a school boy."

Floyd looked up and saw his tormentor prancing about with the spectacles on his face while his two buddies guffawed and slapped themselves on their knees in unbridled laughter.

Cedric leaned down, mockingly smiled at Floyd, and then asked in honeyed tones, "Would you like your glasses back, sweetie?"

Floyd scowled and snarled between clenched teeth, "Give those back to me!"

Cedric straightened up, took the frames off, and said, "Certainly, my good man."

Cedric held out the spectacles but as Floyd grabbed for them, he jerked them back, threw them on the ground, and smashed them to pieces with his big right foot. Then, he grabbed Floyd by the collar, drove two powerful jabs into his face and shoved him to the ground with all his force.

Floyd lay there senseless for several seconds, blood dripping out of his nose onto the dirt. At last, his body jerked spastically, and he came to with a groan. The first thing he saw when he could focus his eyes were the shattered black plastic frames scattered on the ground a few feet away. Floyd put a hand to his nose to staunch the bleeding, and with his other arm dragged himself towards the shards of his magic spectacles. He picked up the fragment of an ear piece and examined it, turning it this way and that in his bloody hand. Then he pulled himself up on an elbow and began to rake together the ruins of his brief academic glory with his gory fingers. As the tears streamed down his cheeks and mingled with the blood from his nose, he heard the raucous laughter of Cedric and his henchmen receding into the distance.

Floyd could not sleep that night. What kept him awake was not the throbbing of his bruised cheek and swollen nose, nor was it the memory of the horrified expression on his mother's face when she arrived home from work and saw his ravaged face. No, it was the bitter realization that the magic eyeglasses, along with the brain power and confidence they had endowed him with, were now gone forever. He was stupid, timid Floyd again, and he would stay that way for the rest of his life. For a few more minutes, he continued to stare into the darkness, the utter hopelessness of his situation dominating his thoughts. He remembered the movie he had watched on TV about the poor boy who ran away, sailed the South Pacific on merchant ships, and eventually returned home to his parents, a triumphant, wealthy sea captain. No future like that awaited him now, just failure and poverty. He could see his mother as an old woman, her grey head bowed down by the gnawing disappointment in her only child.

Floyd reached over and switched on the lamp. After his eyes adjusted to the light, he swung his legs over the edge of the bed, slowly stood up, and trudged over to his desk. There lay the fragments of the magic spectacles that had transformed his life; now they were just a worthless pile of shattered plastic. He picked up the trash can next to the desk and with one motion of his open hand, swept his hopes and dreams into oblivion. It was all over now. With bitter tears streaking down his cheeks, he shuffled back to his bed, turned off the light, and then buried his aching face into the cool softness of the pillow.

When Shamika walked into first period English class the next morning, she started to say *hi* to Floyd, but instead of a cheery greeting, all that escaped her lips was a gasp.

"Floyd, what happened?" she finally blurted out.

Floyd stared at the surface of his desk, then glanced up at his classmate and replied, "I tripped over a curb...fell right on my face."

Shamika plopped down in her seat, her eyes still riveted on Floyd's battered face. She recalled Floyd's amazing transformation from yesterday.

"What happened to your glasses? They seemed to help you concentrate better." she said.

Floyd ran his index finger over the top of the desk a couple of times, then looked over at Shamika and responded, "All busted up from the fall."

Just then Mr. Cahill walked in, placed his briefcase on his desk, and opened his mouth to greet the two early arrivals, but all he could do was gape at Floyd.

"Good grief, Floyd! You look awful. What on earth happened?" he said.

Floyd answered with the exact words he had used to respond to Shamika's query. When Mr. Cahill inquired about the glasses—he had to admit to himself that they had seemed to improve Floyd's academic performance the previous day—Floyd again replied with the exact words he had used before.

It's as if he had rehearsed his answers, Shamika mused. She began to suspect that there was more to the story than Floyd wanted to reveal.

Once the other students had arrived and Mr. Cahill had begun the day's discussion of *A Tale of Two Cities* and in spite of Floyd's stellar performance the day before, he did not contribute anything to today's discussion. Whenever Mr. Cahill asked him a question, Floyd would just shake his head and continue to stare languidly at his open book. Mr. Cahill was utterly perplexed.

How could such a complete metamorphosis occur and relapse from one day to the next? he wondered.

The best explanation he could come up with was that Floyd probably did not feel well because of his injuries.

Maybe he'll perk up by tomorrow, Mr. Cahill thought to himself hopefully.

All morning long Floyd had been dreading geometry, the only class he had with Cedric. He had even been tempted to skip fourth period, but he knew that when his mother found out, she would be even more worried about him than she already was. When Cedric strolled through the door of Mrs. Wilson's classroom and beheld his victim's red, puffy face, he grinned broadly; and, as he sat down in his seat behind Floyd, he slapped him amiably on the back and remarked with a chuckle, "I hear you tripped over a curb and broke your precious glasses."

Floyd cringed but said nothing. Shamika, who had been leafing through her binder to find her geometry homework when Cedric had arrived, had noted both his self-satisfied conviviality and Floyd's reaction to it. Her suspicion deepened. Shamika had known Cedric since the sixth grade and was fully cognizant of his propensity to bully the smaller boys. She assumed Cedric had assaulted Floyd after school to get even with him for the wisecrack he had made about tutoring him in geometry. She had never been a close friend to Floyd, whom she—at least until yesterday—had always considered to be a real dolt. Now, however, she felt that she had to get to the bottom of what had happened to him and his ridiculous eyeglasses. She made up her mind to confront him about it after school.

When Shamika pulled out of the student parking lot—her used car had been a gift from her parents as a reward for being on the first honor roll every six weeks since the seventh grade—she knew exactly where to find Floyd. Every day after school she had passed him trudging down the sidewalk on his way home.

She pulled up beside him, rolled down the passenger-side window and yelled out, "Hey, Floyd! Climb in and I'll give you a ride home."

Floyd's eyebrows shot up; the invitation was so surprising to him that he froze on the spot. Shamika looked around. She did not want any of her friends to see her pick up Floyd and get the wrong idea.

"Get in, Floyd! I don't have all day," she barked.

Floyd managed to regain his composure, hurry over to the car, and hop in. Still fumbling with the seat belt, he glanced at her out of the corners of his eyes and muttered, "Thanks."

After they had ridden a block or two, Shamika pulled into a supermarket parking lot, found a space as far from the front door as possible, and parked the car.

Shamika turned to Floyd and demanded, "What really happened to you? I don't believe that BS about tripping over a curb."

His brow knitted and he stared silently at the floorboard for several seconds.

Finally, he shook his head emphatically and responded, "I can't tell you."

"You mean you won't tell me," Shamika insisted. Then she added, "Well, I'll tell you. Cedric beat you up, didn't he? All 'cause of that wise-crack about tutoring him in geometry."

Floyd shot her a quick glance and an unmistakable expression of fear appeared on his battered face. It was clear to Shamika that he was afraid that Cedric might beat him up again if he thought he had blabbed to her.

Floyd resumed his examination of the floorboard for several seconds. Suddenly, he lifted his head, turned towards Shamika, and blurted out angrily, "To hell with Cedric! I don't give a damn about him. He's just a stupid bully." Then to his own surprise, he added bitterly, "It's the magic glasses. Without them I'm nothin' and I won't never be more than nothin' for the rest of my life."

Immediately, he wished he had not revealed to Shamika what was really bothering him. They were just classmates, not friends. Furthermore, there was nothing she could do to help him. He felt utterly alone and lost.

Shamika was stunned by the vehemence of Floyd's outburst. She thought about what he had said and it occurred to her that Floyd genuinely believed that those plastic frames had transformed him into an intelligent person. She shook her head in astonished disbelief.

"Look, Floyd," she asserted in as calm and soothing a tone as she could muster, "those glasses didn't make you smart. They weren't magic."

Floyd's face darkened and he glared at her.

"Then how did they make me know all that stuff yesterday?" he countered angrily.

Shamika sighed in frustration, gestured towards him with open palms, and replied pointedly, "All those glasses did was give you a sense of confidence in yourself, Floyd, confidence that you never felt before. Once you had a positive view of yourself, you were able to learn."

Floyd's brows rose in surprise, he leaned back and gazed at her in disbelief.

"You're completely wrong!" he exclaimed angrily.

Then he grabbed his backpack, quickly climbed out of the car, and as bitter tears formed in his eyes, snarled, "I'd rather walk home."

Shamika sighed again, shrugged her shoulders in resignation, and muttered to herself, "Oh, well, I tried."

That evening as Floyd sat at his desk puzzling over his geometry homework, he could not help but remember how easy he had found understanding right triangles two evenings ago while he was wearing his magic glasses. He put his pencil down and thought back to the conversation he had had with Shamika after school. He slammed his fist down on his desk in frustration and anger.

She should just mind her own business, he thought to himself bitterly. *Without my magic glasses I can't understand nothin', not now and not ever.*

In spite of this nagging sense of hopelessness, he picked up his pencil and resumed staring blankly at the practice problem he had been trying to solve for the last ten minutes: $a^2 = c^2 - ?$. Suddenly, he recalled the answer he had given Mrs. Wilson yesterday in class. When she had asked what the equation was for the Pythagorean Theorem, he had replied $a^2 + b^2 = c^2$. He looked at the problem again and thought *What was missing?* Immediately, a light flashed on in his brain. The answer had to be b^2. What else could it be? But how did the book get $a^2 = c^2 - b^2$ from $a^2 + b^2 = c^2$? Then a second light flashed on in his brain. Last year in Algebra I, he had learned that whatever you did to one side of an equation, you had to do the same thing to the other side. Of course! If you subtracted b^2 from both sides of $a^2 + b^2 = c^2$, the result had to be $a^2 = c^2 -$

b^2. It seemed so obvious to him now. *Why had he found it so hard?* he thought.

Floyd put his pencil down again, pushed his chair back, and gazed at the wall for a few moments. Then Shamika's words came back to him. She had said that his glasses were not magic at all, that they had just given him the confidence in himself that he had always lacked. *Could that be true?* he wondered. Floyd reached into the trashcan to fish out a couple of pieces of his broken eyeglasses. He held them up in the beam of light from his desk lamp, turning them this way and that to see if any of the old magic had survived their destruction of Cedric's shoe heel. After examining the fragments for a few seconds, he shook his head despondently and tossed them back into the trashcan. Maybe Shamika's right. *Maybe all my magic spectacles did was give me confidence*, he pondered. Floyd pushed his chair back up to the desk, picked up his pencil.

"Well, I guess there's only one way to find out," he said.

The following day in Mrs. Wilson's fourth period geometry class, Shamika kept glancing surreptitiously at Floyd. Earlier in Mr. Cahill's English class, Floyd had been as unwilling to participate in the discussion as he had been yesterday. He had not exhibited so much as a flicker of interest in what was going on around him, and Floyd seemed just as uninterested in the geometry lesson. But true to form, Mrs. Wilson would not give up on him.

"Floyd, if a right triangle has equal legs, how many degrees do each of the other two angles have?" she inquired in her usual hopeful tone of voice.

Floyd could hear Cedric chuckling softly behind him. Shamika figured that Floyd would just shake his head and keep staring blankly at his open book, but to her surprise, Floyd answered Mrs. Wilson.

"Well, I, uh, think each of the angles would have to be, uh, let's see...yes, it would be forty-five degrees," he replied.

Mrs. Wilson was struck mute for a moment.

"That's exactly right, Floyd. Well done!" she remarked with unmistakable delight.

Floyd heard Cedric mutter something under his breath, then he glanced over at Shamika. She nodded and smiled at him and as Floyd grinned at her in return, he felt a surge of pride.

Well, Cedric will probably beat me up again, but he'll never be able to smash my self-confidence. That's for sure, he thought to himself.

Hunting The Sacred Animal, Two Rivers 1916

PATRICK CABELLO HANSEL

My father was a pretty good hunter, which put him at a disadvantage with many of the men in Two Rivers, who were unworldly superb. They may not have been born with rifles in their hands, as Papa says, but I'm convinced they came out of the womb smelling prey two hundred yards away. The Bergerson boys, the Gaineys, and the Swanson twins all could have lived off the land, as long as they had enough bullets or arrows.

Because we lived near Two Rivers, we were near the crossing paths of many animals. Turtles, frogs, and fish were abundant. Deer came down to the streams every night to drink, and there were plenty of rabbits, squirrels, ruffed grouse, turkey, and muskrats. Every other year or so, a feral pig wandered through. Maybe they had burst out of captivity some time back, and when they ran out of things to eat, they came into Two Rivers. It was usually winter, and pigs didn't run well in the snow. It was the custom that whoever shot the poor beast would host a winter barbecue for the whole village.

Maybe there's a world where human beings don't have to kill to survive, but I've never lived there. If done right, taking an animal's life can be a spiritual thing. Elisha Running Bear taught me how the Dakota and the Osage always prayed to the Spirit of the animal they were about to hunt, thanking them for their life. "Without our brother animals, we could not be," she told me many times. She was too old to do much hunting, but neighbors would bring her game. Eating with her always seemed like a prayer.

But killing another being is not a glorious thing, if done the wrong way. I've seen young men from the big town, drunk or sober, ride on horses or drive their fathers' cars on the road between our neighborhood and the cemetery, and shoot at anything that moved. Rose Rank's eldest lost an eye and part of his nose when a bullet ricocheted off the big rock near the gravedigger's shed. Other boys from the town have paid with their lives when they mixed whisky and gunpowder.

I always pushed Papa to let me go on hunts with him, and he always stalled. He never said that a girl couldn't hunt like some of the boys at my school would say when I told them I wanted to go. I think he was afraid that I would get hurt, or worst of all, that he would shoot me, which would have been an unbearable cross for him to bear.

I kept pushing and pushing, but he wouldn't budge. Then on Christmas Day, when I was twelve, one of my presents was wrapped with the most beautiful paper and ribbons. My father had written "Merry Christmas, Rabbit" on it. I couldn't wait to open it, but all I found inside was an old canvas bag with a leather strap that had seen some wear. I said, "Thank you," but I must have shown my disappointment because he walked over to where I sat, put his hand on my shoulder and said,

"Aren't you going to look inside?"

Inside the bag was a folded piece of the *Saturday Evening Post*. It showed a boy sitting by the fireplace with his dog. Beneath the picture were these words: "Make this Christmas 'the best ever' for your boy!" I thought it was some stupid joke. Papa loved to play jokes on us, but this one felt cruel. I've always admitted to being a tomboy, but a tomboy is a girl, and I'm proud of it. I was about to cry when he told me:

"Unfold the rest of it, Graciela."

I did. Written in big red letters were the words "for your girl," with girl underlined and bigger than the other words.

I still didn't get it. I must have said a weak "Thank you" or something, not at all sufficient, because he took the piece of newspaper and held it close to my face.

"What do you see my darling girl? What's in the picture?"

All I saw was this stupid boy in a bathrobe sitting by a stupid fire with his stupid dog. By then, Mama, Jean, and even little Agnes were laughing hard. The more I looked at it; the less I saw. Finally, they all shouted at once:

"Look at the picture, Graciela!"

I looked and then I looked again, and then on the third try, it hit me? the boy was holding a rifle! It was an advertisement for a 1910 Winchester .22 caliber. I jumped up so fast and hugged Papa so hard that I almost knocked over the lamp.

"I'm getting a gun?...I'm getting a gun!"

"Now, it's not a brand new one like the one in the picture," Papa said. "But I think it's time that you and I do a little hunting."

I was so happy that I almost forgot to open my other presents, and to this day, I cannot remember anything else about that Christmas except the promise of a hunting experience.

Minnesota had begun to enact hunting laws prior to 1900, but to be honest, they weren't enforced all that well. Papa had to pay a license fee of one dollar, but I didn't need one?not until I was older. Deer season was supposed to last a single-month?November; and you were supposed to tag the animal right away, but there wasn't exactly a lot of enforcement around Two Rivers, or any other part of the county.

Papa took the rest of the week to teach me?over and over and over? how to be safe with the gun, how to use the gun, how to clean the gun, and how to take the gun apart and put it back together. When it wasn't snowing, we went out walking with our unloaded guns in the woods. He wanted to see how I walked with the gun, and what happened if I stumbled. On the day before New Year's Eve we took practice shots at an old stump. Then, on New Year's Eve, Papa woke me up before dawn. There was a little fog coming up from a turtle?evidence that it was going to be a gray day. He told me to put on two pairs of pants, two pairs of socks, and to quietly come downstairs. When I got to the kitchen he gave me a cup of coffee and a piece of bread with preserves on it.

"Is this all we're going to eat for breakfast?" I asked.

"This isn't breakfast, chipmunk," he said. "This is just a little something to get our stomach going. It's best to not go hunting with an empty stomach because you'll be too edgy; and never go hunting with a full stomach because you'll be slow and want to go sit down to digest somewhere. But a little food in the stomach keeps you hungry, but not desperate. Desperate hunting is not good for you or for the animal."

"Why's that?" I asked.

"Because if you're desperate you can get jumpy, and if you're jumpy, you're more likely to wound an animal rather than kill it. A wounded animal that gets away from you is likely to suffer a slow, terrible death."

That took some of the shine off of my first hunt, but my demeanor picked up again as we put on our boots and coats, picked up our guns, and stepped outside. I couldn't see the sun through the low, gray clouds, but I could tell it was starting to get lighter.

"Where are we going?" I asked him.

"I think the woods west of the cemetery would be a good place to start," he said. "There's only one farm up there and Mr. Carlson has let me hunt there many times. There's a slough and a bit of a bog that will be frozen over that we can cross."

When we walked through Two Rivers, no one was up and about. We saw no lamps or candles in any house. However, it would be very different on New Year's Eve when every house would be lit and we would all gather for a bonfire near the Big Oak. When we got to the road near the cemetery, I could see the fog shrouding the Turtle. It came up around the bridge like it was almost a little band of ghosts. I knew better than to mention ghosts because that would have started Papa on an extra long series of stories about ghosts, spirits, and "crossing between," and then we'd never get any hunting done.

We walked through the cemetery. It was kind of strange carrying our guns through the resting place of so many dead. I used to mushroom hunt there with Agnes, and sometimes I would go to just sit in the cemetery and think. Yet here we were, walking through an "eternal resting place" with our instruments of death, as if we owned the place (or at least the destination). I assume St. Adalbert's, located in town, legally owned the land?but to me, a cemetery is one place where the concept of "ownership" doesn't seem to matter. After we passed through the cemetery, I asked my father about the buried:

"Papa, do you think the dead like us walking through their land with our guns?"

He turned his head and looked at me.

"That's a really good question, Graciela. What do you think?"

I expected him to have a long and complex answer, so I had to think for a while.

"Well, I don't know," I said. "If they are listening—if they *can* listen, they probably hear a lot of people walking around and a lot of talking."

"And they probably hear a lot of people crying as well," he said.

"None of our kin are buried there, are they?"

"No."

"Do you know where some of our ancestors are buried?" I asked.

"Well, there's some of my ancestors buried in Louisiana, and some of your Mama's are buried in Mexico and south Texas, and then there are some that were never buried and instead died at sea or in the desert."

"Do you think that our ancestors get lonely sometimes?"

He stopped and turned his whole body towards me.

"Why all these questions about the dead, Graciela?" he asked. "Are you worried about something?"

"No...it's just that sometimes...maybe I shouldn't tell you this, but sometimes I sit in the cemetery and talk to the people buried there. Is that bad?"

He took his gun in his right hand, leaned it down toward the ground, and put his left hand on my shoulder.

"No, Graciela, a lot of people do that; probably more than you think."

"But, Papa, what if the dead start talking to me?"

I didn't tell him that that had already happened—or at least, I thought it had happened. I don't know how I expected him to react and was nervous he would look at me as if I was strange. I knew that Elisha Running Bear communicated with spirits and so did Señora Herrera. I asked Mom if she experienced anything like that, and she just said, "Some things we speak on the inside and we do not speak them aloud." That statement made me think that she had the same gift, and that maybe I was special.

But Papa didn't look worried or upset. Instead, he looked as if an encounter with the dead was the most natural thing in the world.

"I think that if the dead start talking to you, Graciela, the best thing you can do is to listen."

Then he nodded at me—as if he understood; as if he wasn't going to say anything else about it; as if it was okay.

We walked through Mr. Carlson's corn field, where a few dry stalks stood above the snow, and then crossed over the frozen slough. We were almost to the woods when I heard a loud shot ring out. It took me a few seconds to realize that my dad had shot at something, which was why the sound was so loud.

"What did you shoot at, Papa ?" I asked.

"A rabbit!" he said "but I missed it. Look! There's another one! You take the shot."

The rabbit had paused by a little clump of grass that stood above the snow—as if he thought that he couldn't be seen there. Time seemed to slow down. I raised my rifle, got the little critter in sight, and breathed in deeply. Papa had told me over and over to squeeze the trigger—not pull it. He told me to breathe all the air out before I fired, and I shot the rifle exactly the way he taught me. As I felt the gunstock recoil against my shoulder, I saw the rabbit jump in the air and fall over.

"You got it, Graciela! You got it!" Papa shouted. "Let's go get it!"

We ran over the snow to the rabbit, which was about forty yards away. When we got there, I could see its blood on the snow and on its sandy-colored fur. Its back legs kicked, one harder than another. Its breathing was strange, and it looked like it was trying to run away, trying to get to safety, but it couldn't.

"It's wounded badly," Papa said. "Graciela, you must put it out of its misery."

"How, Papa? I can't shoot it again. We're too close."

He looked at me and said, "You have to pick it up and wring its neck."

"No Papa, no!" I cried. "I can't do it! That would be too cruel."

He laid his gun down on a stump, and took both of my arms with his big hands.

"No, Graciela, it would be cruel to let it suffer," he said.

"Look at it. Is that what you want it to go through?"

"No, Papa, I don't want it to suffer," I said, "but I can't hurt it like that."

"Graciela, you already hurt it. You shot it."

I started crying.

"You do it Papa," I said. "I can't touch that poor little thing."

He grabbed my arms even tighter and looked at me sternly.

"Daughter, this is what it means to hunt. You took this creature's life. You made the shot. Now its life is seeping out and you can't save it, but you can spare it some pain at the end of its life."

I knew I had to do it, but I was shaking so hard that I didn't think I could.

"Give me your gun, Graciela," Papa said. "You can do this. You are stronger than you think."

I picked up the poor thrashing rabbit, and got blood on my gloves and my coat. I tried to look away from it, but I couldn't. It was still kicking in my arms, slower, but still kicking. I looked at my father, and then I looked at the rabbit, then I cried out, "I'm sorry, Mr. Rabbit, please forgive me."

As his neck snapped, something rose up in me, something words couldn't describe. I looked to my father, then I looked up at the sky. A hawk soared overhead. Maybe the hawk thought I couldn't go through with it, and would leave the rabbit for him.

"Put the rabbit in your game bag," Papa said.

I loosened the leather drawstring on the bag that hung off my hip—the same bag Papa had given me for Christmas. The bag didn't feel like a cheerful gift anymore.

Papa asked me if I wanted to keep on hunting or go back home. I looked at him for a long time. The rabbit was my first kill—my first good shot. I knew it would not be my last experience with death, but it was enough for one day.

"Let's go back," I said.

Most of the way back we didn't talk. Papa decided to avoid the cemetery and walked around it. When we finally got to the road, he said:

"If you need to relieve yourself, go to the outhouse right away. Then I'll show you how to skin and gut the rabbit so we can eat it for dinner."

I knew that he would make me skin and gut the rabbit, and I also knew that such tasks were part of hunting. It was my shot, my kill, and therefore, I needed to take responsibility for it. As I skinned and gutted my little rabbit, I prayed. The prayer started as one of grief and remorse for taking another creature's life, but as I worked, it transformed into a prayer of thanksgiving and of compassion. I finally understood what it meant to take a life in order to preserve life, and I gave thanks to my father for requiring me to participate in every aspect of hunting.

Mama cooked the rabbit for supper that night along with onions, potatoes, and carrots from the root cellar. Of course, I'd eaten rabbit before, but eating the rabbit I shot made me feel sad. I ate it anyway because it would have been a slap in the face of the sacred not to do so since the animal had given up his life to feed me and my family. It felt complicated—I was proud of my shot, scared of the power of death, and sad that a creature expired at my hands. But I was not alone—we were all there: me, Papa, Mama, Jean, and Agnes, the rabbit, Two Rivers, and the land. We were all made out of the same stuff, and there was no way I wanted to tear that apart.

Into the Frame

ROBERT HARRINGTON

There is a routine to grief. The counting of the days since it came. The 16 steps to the kitchen for coffee, the 13 intrusive memories, the three minutes it takes to brush my teeth before I go to sleep, to dream, to wake, and then to repeat. After loss, you can't help but see your life for what it is. A brief, perpetual motion machine that runs on the lie that the engine will always turn.

It's been days since I left our apartment. I know it can't stay this way, but the places I went to while you were still here are now misshapen and odd, as if the moment you died someone erected a replica of the city. Maybe this is why I won't go see Allison. It's been weeks since I have, and when I do, I have nothing to say. Talking to her makes me feel like the version of her I loved, the one who was your friend and my girlfriend—in that order—is gone, and the one that remains is just a reenactment; as false as old men dressing as Confederate soldiers, choosing to remember history how they want. I shouldn't be like this, but I am.

I got the text from Jim yesterday. He wants to meet up at our old bar to talk about you. It took me hours to reply "yes" and when I did, I regretted it. I know he meant something to you, but I know what that meaning did to you—where it helped lead you.

I take two steps into the bar, and a riptide of nostalgia pulls me across the room—to my red booth; to your profanity-carved table; to our spot. I take our table for two in the back and wait. The waitress who comes is round with red cheeks. She's dressed in a faded blue skirt and a once-white, now yellow, button-up shirt. I hate her without a second thought.

"What'll you have?" she asks, flakes of dry saliva flickering off her lips, chapped by a pack-a-day habit and a steady diet of soda and beer.

"Whiskey."

"What kind?"

"The kind that doesn't cost ten dollars." She gives me a terse look that would rival your mother's and walks away. After that response, she'll give me a bottom-shelf and charge me a premium. It's what I deserve, and the Xanax I took on the bus over keeps me from caring. There's no real reason to hate her. There's never a good reason to hate anyone on sight, but I do, I hate her.

I watch her walk away, and I run my fingers through the grooves of the carved words on your table.

Get High

LOVE

No Gods No Masters

Dave sucks

I can't remember which one of these you carved, but you never cared for being sentimental, and, as far as I know, you've never known a Dave.

The bar is different now. Instead of the usual working-class drunks, it's now infested with "brunchers" corralling their children as they softly sip five-dollar Bloody Marys, being careful not to drink too much to avoid making a scene. You would hate it. I hate it.

Getting here early was a mistake. I still don't know what I'm going to do when Jim gets here and now I can't stop thinking about everyone we knew. Funny how our friends moved in such opposite directions—some living on the top floor of those surging condos and some resting under a door frame, strung out south of the city center. He's going to ask about you. He's going to inquire, and I'm going to dodge the question. What can I say that hasn't already flurried around our old friends? He wants details of his own to spread, to tantalize a dinner party with a story about his "old" friends and his "old" life. I wonder if

they know who he was. I wonder if they know about the constant sup-
ply of coke he pushed up the nostrils of eighteen-year-old girls, new to
the city, unaware of what people like him will do to them. I wonder if
he tells them about his grandfather's money putting him into rehab and
then into that condo. I wonder if he tells them about you. I wonder
if he tells them about denying you to everyone. I wonder if he tells
them about denying himself. You always did pick wrong: straight boys
in khakis, straight boys in polos, straight boys picking at their curiosity.
The perils you faced with every meeting would have crushed me. Simple
attraction couldn't guide you. It often broke you. You must've hated me
a little. I could walk into a bar, see a girl, like a girl, and then, with a little
small talk, maybe be with that girl. The propositions I make are usually
only met with approval or denial, rarely aggression.

Jim walks in, dressed in a clean, fitted navy suit. God, money does
look good on everyone. I dip my head and pretend not to see him walk
through the door. Turning my head to the right, I lift my glass to cover
my face as he walks toward my direction. Finally, I put my glass down
and feign surprise when he joins my table. I regret this more already.

"Hey, how's it going?" There's an excitement in his voice that seems
wrong, considering the reason for our meeting.

"Good, how are you doing?"

"I'm doing alright. I'm still in shock. I'm sorry to hear about Ben,"
Jim says, putting on his best frown.

"Well, it's been over a month."

"I know, but I just found out."

"Really, I thought that the word would spread pretty quickly."

I can't buy this. I can't believe that he's here to catch up, to talk about
you, to have some kind of impromptu wake in the back of this shitty
bar. I can't believe he's sorry.

"Yeah, but I'm not in that crowd anymore. It took me a week to get
your number after I found out."

"Still got the same number."

"Yeah, I got a new phone. Lost my contacts."

I decide to accept this and move on. He's committed, and I'm too tired. The waitress wobbles over, pulling her notebook from the constraints of her apron pocket.

"Hi, what'll you have?"

"I'll have a Bloody Mary."

She smiles, pleased with his order. She looks over to me and I point to my glass. There's no use for pretense. She doesn't like me, and I don't like her. The less words exchanged the better.

"So, what else have you been up to?" Jim asks.

His question makes me want to reach over and grab him by the throat.

"Since the funeral?"

"Yeah."

"Not much. You know how it is." It's a simple response, but it's the only one I can muster.

"You're still working at The Public House?"

"Yep, I'm the sous-chef now."

This isn't true. At least I don't think it is. I haven't shown up to work in weeks.

"Cool, I love their sandwiches. God, we used to eat there every time we went drinking. It's been forever since I've been. I'm working for my grandfather now. Just got promoted. It's a sweet job—company car, expense account, I even have a secretary."

"Living the dream." Jim doesn't catch my sarcasm. He just nods and flips through his phone for a moment before setting it back down. The waitress brings our drinks and hurries away.

"You know it. I mean, it blows having to do the nine to five thing, but Samantha digs it. You should see it when I come home. She's just waiting by the door. She's practically panting. She loves the suits. I finally started getting them tailored. I didn't realize how much better it makes you look. You can't buy off the rack. Makes you look like a schlep. You should go to a tailor when you start having to wear 'em. He's a little handsy, but the guy is 'in fashion,' if you know what I mean." Jim pulls the celery away from the rim of his glass and drinks. A crimson red drips from both corners of his mouth.

"Got to look the part." I only have one suit and it hangs off of me, but I don't give a shit.

"Are you seeing anybody?" Jim asks, putting his drink on a cork coaster.

"Yeah, been seeing someone for about six months."

"Wow, six months? That must be some sort of record. Well, I guess, it kind of makes sense. It's got to be easier now."

"What do you mean?" I ask, finally letting my voice raise.

Jim notices it and slumps back in his chair, raising his palms out in front of him.

"I didn't mean it like that. But, you know, it must be easier. You can't keep a girl too long if you're pseudo-married to your best friend. You can't do that shit when you're our age. Chicks want you to be all about them—all about Eve. You can't go ditching them to hang out with the serpent in the garden."

"The serpent? What the fuck is that supposed to mean?"

I'm going to do it. I'm going to reach across this table and throttle him. I'm going to give him and all the "brunchers" a story. I'm going to be the subject of whispers.

"I didn't mean it like that. Fuck, you know I didn't. I was just running my mouth. I was friends with him too, you know."

"Oh, I know. I know you two were friends. He always told me who his friends were."

Jim's eyes flutter back and forth, surprised I know. This was supposed to be your guys' little secret, but I don't care. If you wanted it kept, you should be here.

"Hey, I don't know what he told you, but it was never like that. I knew he always had a crush on me. Sure, he came onto me but I didn't go all 'caveman' on him about it. Maybe he misunderstood that. I mean, shit, I have a fiancé now. I would never."

His voice shakes and I feel sorry for him. I let it go; he's built a box for himself and it isn't my place to tear at it. I lie and say I didn't mean it. I say I'm just drunk.

"It's okay. I get it," he says before exhaling softly across the table as he fingers the rim of his drink, looking down at the table.

My phone buzzes in my pocket. I apologize out of habit and check the text. It's from Allison. It's the fourth one today. I haven't replied back to any of them, and the frequency with which she is texting makes me regret that, but I can't reply, let alone answer her calls. God, Allison loved you. I think the only reason she started dating me was because you were around. When the three of us would walk to the store, she would let go of my hand and wrap her arms around you. The two of you were always five steps ahead of me, whispering and laughing. I remember it for what it was—a beautiful picture, and when you walked, everyone would move out of your way, careful not to break into the frame. I don't think you ever knew I noticed when Allison would slip out of bed to be with you when you couldn't sleep. You two would laugh and have all these secret jokes and when I asked you what they were about, you would never tell. I don't think I ever really wanted to know. I still don't. I like that there is still something I don't know about you. Something about you I could still learn. If you were here, you'd tell me to quit being such a dick and text her back. I will. Later. I promise, but first I have to get out of here.

"Sorry about that," I say, putting my phone back in my pocket.

I must have been looking at it for a while because Jim is almost done with his drink.

"No worries. Anyways, I have to go. I'm having dinner with some friends at my place," Jim says, looking at his phone.

I nod and we both begin to stand as Jim reaches out his arms. My legs wobble and I take a half step back. A hug? Really? When were we ever "hug" friends? But this is what people do in times like this. They foster intimacy. An intimacy unneeded in happier times. Tragedy is a shared event, and everyone wants to insert themselves into its awful narrative, to be a key player on a shitty stage. I throw a twenty on the table and put on my coat as Jim and I walk out of the bar into a light rain. It's nearly winter in Seattle and the gold of the fall litters the streets. We shake hands and promise to meet up again, you know, sometime. The "I'll call you" charade. Jim walks north up Ballard Avenue and I go south. I walk slowly, a few steps behind a tall man and beautiful woman. I keep my distance, careful not to break into the frame.

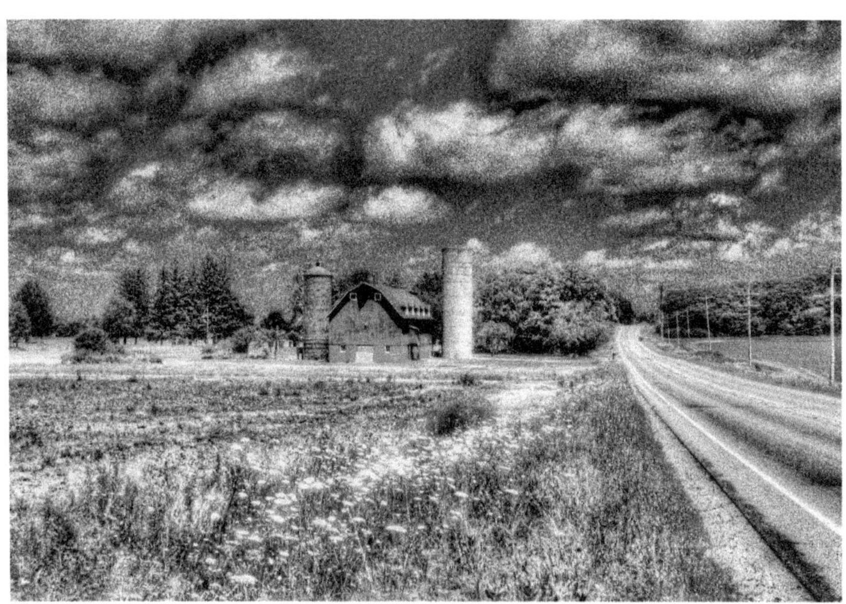

Digital photograph with post-processing modifications
David S. Rubenstein

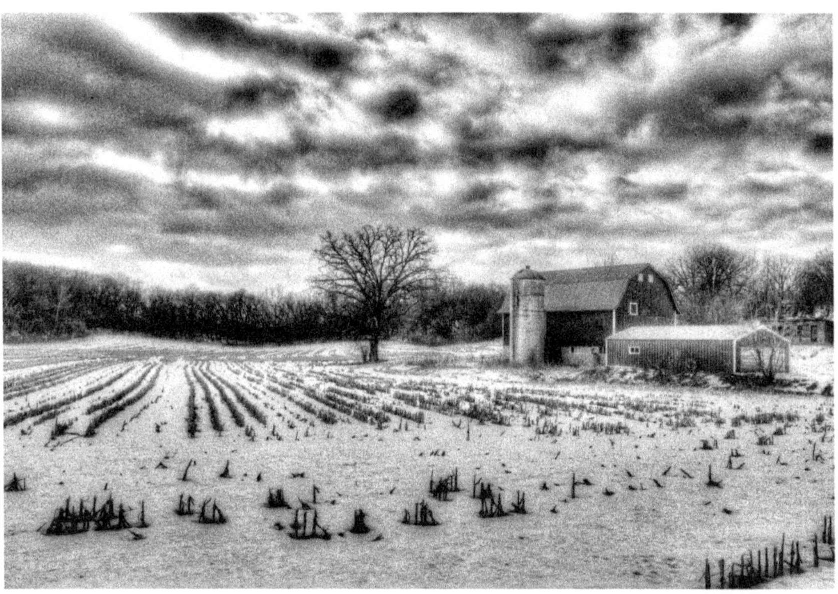

Digital photograph with post-processing modifications
David S. Rubenstein

Off Broadway

HILARY WHEELAN REMLEY

The idea had been to escape the city. Jamie had her novel to work on, and Russell was itching for the baby to see a bit of nature. So they rented a house in Saratoga, a nice, non-air-conditioned Queen Anne close to downtown. But so far, they had not ventured anywhere farther than the racecourse. Instead, they held up in the house where they took turns sitting in the kiddy pool out back, and arguing in whispers so as not to wake the baby during her naptime.

They developed a habit of getting ice cream whenever they reached a point where they were about to file for divorce. Jamie had gone up two pants sizes so far and it was only July.

The line into Ben & Jerry's ® extended out the front door. Russell grabbed a menu from inside and brought it over to read.

"Chunky Mon-KEY?" Russell asked, tickling the baby's stomach. The baby wiggled at her side, slipping low on Jamie's hip.

"Mah-mah," the baby said.

"They're out," Jamie pointed to the X over the flavor on the board above the register. She shifted the baby up higher on her hip.

"Okay," Russell said, "how about Cherry Gar-see-YAH?"

The baby looked at him with rapt attention. "Chewwy."

"Cherry?" He smiled. "Jamie, she said cherry. That's thirty words! Can you say cherry?"

The baby said nothing.

They moved in the line for some time, not saying anything, until it was nearly their turn to order.

"What flavor do you want?" Jamie asked.

"Next," the cashier said, waving them over.

"I'll have a scoop of pistachio in a waffle cone," Jamie said, fishing her wallet from her purse. She looked at Russell, who was in the middle of stealing the baby's nose. "And two scoops of Cherry Garcia for them, in a cup."

"Actually," Russell said, returning the baby's nose to her plump little face, "this lady will have a scoop of vanilla in a cup. I'll have a scoop of cookie dough in a cone."

"How cute," the cashier said, "aren't you two just so cute?"

Jamie stalked out to an open gazebo while Russell waited for the ice cream. She sat with the baby and bounced her up and down on her shaking knee, and looked out over to a group of women all dressed in burgundy and crepe cocktail dresses, all fanning their contoured faces. One of them was crying, carefully blotting her eyes with tissue. It was three in the afternoon and she'd already spotted four weddings clumped around the innards of Congress Park.

When Russell arrived, he took the baby from Jamie's lap and sat her down on the floor with her cup of ice cream. The baby used her hand to scoop out the little vanilla mound of ice cream from her bowl and toss it at Jamie's knee, hitting it like a bullseye.

"God damn it," Jamie said, grabbing wet wipes from her tote. "Can't you just feed her?"

Russell opened his mouth to retort but stopped short, smacking his lips tight together, as if to say, *I'm not sinking to your level, Jamie.* He sat down on the gazebo floor next to the baby and offered her a lick of his cookie dough.

Russell believed that the baby was special. He didn't want to stifle her spirit—or something like that. His middle name was Phoenix, which she didn't know until they'd gone to apply for their marriage license. Russell went to schools upstate that believed in "unlearning" and "barn-sleeping"—and as he liked to remind Jamie, he'd turned out just fine. "Children needed to be free to play," he said, which isn't an excuse that our landlord would accept in lieu of payment for his crayon swirled walls.

After a few minutes, bees gathered at the pool of vanilla ice cream that had dripped down from her knee and melted at her ankles. Jamie watched Russell and the baby, both sticky, sitting happy as pigs in shit on the gazebo floor as they took turns burying their faces in his ice cream. It was always that way with those two, even when the baby was very little. Russell could play peek-a-boo and she just couldn't. She'd tried once, but only made the baby cry. Russell said it was because the baby could tell that she wasn't really smiling, just making a face.

She watched them and tried to imagine herself sitting next to them on the floor—eating ice cream with her hands, but she couldn't. She got up and threw out her scoop of pistachio, which had begun to melt and drip down her fingers.

"I'm going to the bookstore," she said.

"We're going to look at the duckies in the park," Russell responded.

"Okay," she said.

"Okay," he retorted, then she left.

She rinsed her hands off in a spring, headed down the backside of Broadway, her throat clamped tight around an uncomfortable feeling.

The bookstore was the only place in Saratoga that Jamie liked. It was large but tightly packed, spanning several rooms, each sitting at a slightly different level and linking up in ways that didn't make even the least bit of sense.

She liked just being there. It was quiet—people kept their voices to a whisper, pointed out books, and some said incorrect things about them in such a way as to indicate their own intelligence. She spent hours there shuffling along one wall or another, picking up books and reading pages at random. It was where she went when ice cream failed to work its magic, and she knew the owner by first name.

She came there hoping to unlock something. She thought that a line might strike her in a certain way and she would be motivated to finish writing her own book—she wasn't even close. Her writing, Russell said, in his polite but circular way, was stiff. He'd also said that her character felt like half-melted wax figures, and that there were no school-aged children in America named Tobias.

Russell was a writer, too—he knew what he was talking about. His novels sold reasonably well, better than her single, lowly, short story collection.

She read once, in a book maybe, that two writers could never survive a relationship together—only one of them could come out of the thing alive. She thought of Zelda Fitzgerald clutching her pair of ballet shoes as fire licked at her cell door. But Jamie reasoned that, at this point, she could only half consider herself a writer, so maybe there was hope after all.

Today, she started in the history section. She noticed a disturbing amount of Hitler biographies in used bookstores, all of them, with an unsettling amount of wear. It reminded her of Donahue, one of her many stepfathers. He read *Mein Kampf* every year or so "for research" and spent hours listening to German language learning tapes in the car. Donahue was an accountant so Jamie had no idea what he used such "research" for. Donahue liked to call her mom *hausfrau*, a term which her mother endured only as long as it took to hire a decent and affordable attorney. And once, when Jamie was only thirteen, Donahue told her she had "good, child-bearing hips." Of all of her mother's husbands, she thought of Donahue the most. She'd been trying to write him into her novel but couldn't quite get a grip on him. None of her friends could figure out whether she was trying to make him into a joke or not. Russell's mother, upon reading her first five chapters, had asked her quite bluntly if she had "been touched." She'd said that it would explain a lot about Jamie's personality. Jamie felt that no one really got the point of Donahue's character. She didn't understand why people couldn't be both funny and horrible.

For Russell's part, he never found an issue with her character's likability, but he was always going on about the "why" of it all.

"I need to know that there is something moving them along," he had said, "other than plot."

The topic of her novel had come up, while they were eating dinner at a restaurant called Machiavelli on the West Side. The whole place was decorated with nightmarish decor— with heavy curtains and velvet chairs and such. Russell's cheeks were flushed red from three glasses of wine and he seemed bold. His publisher had just given him his largest advance yet, and things were looking up for him. They ordered panna cotta for dessert and he fell asleep in the back of the cab.

Jamie didn't understand Russell's comment about the plot, and she felt like a student in one of his workshops as she listened to the lecture he gave on "motivation." *Whatever*," Jamie thought. She didn't particularly like the word "motivation." She put him to bed that night and turned him on his side, propped up by pillows on both sides.

"Shit happens," she responded, as she balanced her wedge of panna cotta on the back of her spoon. She liked that saying.

Her mother once got the saying airbrushed to a pair of matching t-shirts in Gulf Shores. This was shortly after her divorce from Donahue and they were celebrating Jamie's sixteenth birthday. They rented a shitty hotel room on the beach and spent every day blitzed on Piña Coladas and Peach Schnapps. Forrest Gump came on TV the second to last day they spent there and her mom broke down and cried over the slogan.

"Shit happens," she'd said, as she paddled her hands in her bathwater that had turned tepid—"and then you die."

Jamie took her to the souvenir shop to cheer her up—it worked. Her mom got the custom shirts made while Jamie went to look at the hermit crabs.

Anyway, that was kind of the point of her book; but apparently, she was bad at saying it. She surmised she'd been standing at the Hitler books for too long when an old man pushed past her to clutch himself a copy. She moved along to another room.

She stopped in the fiction section for a while, it was both cozy and neglected, a place where she could sit for a while without being interrupted. No one collects paperbacks of *Eat, Pray, Love* or *Bridget Jones's Diary*. She took a stack of old *Paris Reviews* from the top shelf and sat down on a step stool, and skimmed each issue to see if anything awful had snuck its way in.

She ended up finding an interview with Paula Fox from the Summer 2004 issue. It was all about her terrible, turbulent childhood, and about how she pinged from one corner of the country to another. She'd spent some time in Cuba before the revolution. It reminded Jamie of her own childhood, even if her own dramas were a little bit less grand. She had spent the majority of her childhood following her mother and her string of ridiculous husbands and boyfriends: Donahue the Nazi, Chet the bodybuilder, and Crispin the Marie Osmand doll collector. They all had strange habits—some had rules against smoking in the house, eating on the couch, and shoes on the carpet. Jamie had liked some but hated most, and never ventured too close to any of them. One way or another, they all wound up wrestling with her mother over a bottle of Wild Turkey.

Jamie remembered her mother standing alongside the dance floor at her own wedding, and how she looked at Jamie with a huge smile. Her mother was single then—she had given up on men around the same time she'd given up on alcohol. Half her teeth were missing, they had rotted from smoking, and her hair was gone from chemotherapy; but she was sober. She didn't drink one lick of alcohol at Jamie's wedding.

"Look," she'd said, when Jamie came over to her table. "Look how good I'm doing." Then she smiled a big, gap-toothed grin, which reminded Jamie of a little kid's.

The ache in Jamie's throat returned, thinking about her mom, and she put down the magazine. She pressed her fingers to the sides of her throat and tried to massage the feeling loose, but really the only way to get rid of it was to cry, and there was no way to stop it at this point. So she clamped her eyes shut, lifted her chin to the ceiling, and let out big catfish wallops of silent sobs.

"Hello," a voice said. "Don't cry." It was a small voice.

She opened her eyes. A little boy stood in front of her, holding out a feather. "Don't cry," he said again. "You can have my feather."

Jamie smiled. The feather was long, white, and the tip was wet with the boy's saliva.

"Cillian," a woman snapped, as she leaned her head over the aisle where Jamie sat. "Don't talk to strangers," she said.

The woman reached her hand out to the little boy. Jamie figured she looked like a mess—dangerous if not traumatizing for a child to look at.

"And drop that feather," the woman said, taking the boy's hand. "It'll give you diseases."

The boy turned away from her and went back to his mother. He dropped the feather on the floor. Jamie stood up and went over to pick it up. She brought the feather back to the bench and played with it a little. Jamie had not yet named the main character her own novel. She named her something different in each draft, sometimes it was Daisy or Carrie or Lizzie, but in each version her character liked to collect feathers. She included this detail because of *Forrest Gump*. In the book she watches *Forrest Gump* and becomes obsessed with finding feathers. And in the final scene, she planned that her main character would run away from home after a particularly bad fight between her mom and the "Donahue-like" character. Instead of a note, she leaves a box of feathers on her bed for her mom to find—it's supposed to be poetic.

But Russell didn't like the ending. He believed that the main character would never run away.

"From the chapters you've shown me, she isn't the type to just up and leave," he said.

But, Jamie wanted to tell him he was wrong. The main character did leave. She did leave—and she knew, because the main character was based on her own life. No, she hadn't run away. She got a scholarship to a college up north instead. She chose that school out of four other schools, two of which were close to home in Georgia, specifically to leave her mother behind.

By then her mother was no longer sober, but she was single. Once, during a vulnerable moment, she asked Jamie not to go. She actually grabbed onto her ankles at the bus station and begged her not to leave.

"I need you," she said. "We could go to the beach."

Jamie was the type to run away. She had already done so, in fact, it didn't matter what Russell had to say on the matter.

Jamie and Russell paid for her mother's hospice, and Jamie called her every day. When her mother finally died, after a five-year stint of cancer, Jamie went down to South Carolina and planned the funeral by herself. Russell was on the road for his book tour. She told him that it was fine, that she could manage on her own, and he believed her. Few people attended the wake, a cousin and two of her hospice nurses, both of whom went up to Jamie and told her just how much her mother gloated over her

"Look," one of them said, holding out a copy of *Rough Edges*, her short story collection. "She gave a copy to anyone who walked in her room. She was so proud of you."

The anecdote was supposed to make her feel better. It didn't.

That night, she went to a bar and ordered a whiskey and coke to ease the ache in her throat. She ended up sleeping with a bartender named Dustin who, in the morning, tried to make her easy mac for breakfast, but ended up setting his microwave on fire when he failed to water to the mix.

She came back from the funeral and Russell gave her a bear hug at the airport. He had just finished his book tour and was in a good mood. They split two bottles of wine and she pressed her face into his neck and cried for two straight hours before they had sloppy, woozy living room floor sex.

And then, a month and a half later, she blacked out in the shower, fell, and split her head on the faucet. Russell found her thirty minutes later with pruned skin and purple lips.

"Head wounds tend to bleed," the nurse to Russell's concerns.

The doctor spent only five minutes in her room before he announced, "You're pregnant; fainting spells can happen."

Upon hearing the news, Russell wept with joy.

That's when the throbbing in her throat really started. That's when she knew that her mother had been right. *Shit happens. You fuck a bartender and shit happens. Hadn't that been how she came to be?* Jamie thought.

Jamie slipped the feather into her pocket and got up. She checked her phone.

"Back home," a text from Russell read. He'd also sent a picture of the baby napping on the couch. She looked so sweet—her face flushed pink from the heat, her mouse-brown hair curled all around her face; she reminded Jamie of herself at that age. She even slept in the same splayed-limb fashion. Jamie could spend hours watching her sleep. Even in the early days, when Jamie herself couldn't be plucked from bed. Even when Russell started feeding the baby from bottles and had to call in help from Jamie's mother upstate.

Jamie went back to the front of the store, near the children's section to pick something up for the baby, maybe a picture book like *Green Eggs and Ham* or *Madeline* to read before bed. Instead, all she found were rows and rows of yellow-spined Nancy Drews.

She looked through the shelves, desperate for anything other than *The Mystery of the Old Clock*, when she came across a copy of *Anne of Green Gables*. The front cover was nearly torn off. It was the edition that her mother used to read to her—it was the one with Megan Follows on the cover, waiting for her new family at the train station with her carpet-bag.

Jamie remembered the first time she watched *Anne of Green Gables* special on PBS. She was little, and sick with the chicken pox. Her mom put in a blank VHS to record the show before she went off to work.

"Oh this is my favorite," she'd said, smoking her morning cigarette.

Jamie had watched the first portion before falling into a fever sleep. When her mother came home later that afternoon, she'd found her crying. Jamie was upset because she had dreamed of Matthew Cuthbert and how he had died in a field in Anne's arms. Her mother tried to comfort her. It wasn't the end of the story, after all.

Jamie's mother found the full set of books over the course of many Goodwill trips and read them all to her. No matter what was going on, Jamie could count on her mother to come into her bedroom at night to read a chapter at a time. She remembered, her breath smelled like red wine. Her lips had a nearly black ring in the center, and Jamie liked to watch the ring expand and contract as she read from the book. Jamie remembered a big, grasping need for her mother in those days. She spent so much time alone in her room, and her mother was often away. She needed something to grab onto.

Jamie wondered when their relationship had turned around. Jamie had felt guilty when her mother called and she did not answer. She felt guilty at her mother's lonely, sparse funeral. Especially when she realized that her mother had held onto her, and was so proud of her. As a little girl, Jamie had yearned for soft, fatherly love like that shown by Matthew Cuthbert, and unlike his character in the book, Jamie's mother had not died in his daughter's arms. And where was she? She had not died in Jamie's arms. A nurse named Amber had found her after she'd been flatlining for over ten minutes. She was alone. She was alone. She was alone.

Shit happens. And then you die.

When she looked at the baby she felt that same need. She was always reaching out to her, calling for her. Her first words, according to Russell, had been Mama. She'd spent that night crying in the tub.

She wondered when things had gone so wrong, why she couldn't hold her baby without feeling a little sad. Maybe that's just how it was.

She bought the book and walked home.

When she got back to the house she found Russell and the baby in the backyard. Russell had a can of beer in his hands and he watched the baby as she splashed in her small plastic pool. Jamie sat down next to Russell and reached her hand out to him for a sip of his beer, which he handed to her without saying a word.

"Did you guys have fun?" she asked.

"I don't know," he said, calling out to the baby. "Did we have fun, Ruthie?"

"Duckies!" Ruthie called back, splashing her arms in the water.

"Did she just learn a new word?" asked Jamie.

He nodded, "she loved the duckies," he said.

They sat together for a minute in silence.

"I'm sorry," she said.

Russell nodded again, "It's ok," he said.

Jamie's throat clenched again and her chin warbled. Russell wrapped his arm around her shoulder.

"I'm sorry," she said, pressing her nose into his chest.

Ruth stopped paddling in her pool. "Mama," she said, as she reached out her hands out to Jamie. Jamie wiped the budding tears away from her eyes, picked the baby up, and carried her over to the steps. Jamie pulled the feather from her pocket and tickled its tip against Ruth's little button nose until she scrunched her shoulders up in insufferable laughter.

"Duckie," Ruth said, grabbing the feather. She turned it around and tickled Jamie's face in slow strokes.

Jamie smiled and repeated back, "Duckie." Ruth climbed down from her lap with the feather and plopped back into the kiddie pool.

"What have you been up to?" Russell asked, brushing Jaimie's hair off her face.

"I bought Ruth a book," she said. She pulled the tattered copy of *Anne of Green Gables* from her purse.

"I think she's still a few words shy of getting that one," he said. Russel kissed Jamie's forehead.

"I know," she said. "But I think she will love it one day."

One More Hug

BRODIE LOWE

She took my keys when I got back home that night. She threatened to kick me out of the house if I didn't get my act together.

***

I was upside down. My palms were open above my head, knuckles resting on the ceiling of the truck. My brain was pounding. I kept saying that I was sorry. *Sorry for missing the road. Sorry for not seeing the deer in time. Sorry I almost killed myself.* I knew someone was out there in the night. I could smell diesel. I heard feet running and I opened my eyes.

A guy squatted down on the shoulder of the road and brought a flashlight up to my face. He scratched his chin with the palm of his hand.

"That you, John?"

"It's me," I said as I squinted and shielded my eyes with my hand, which had fallen asleep.

It was Cedric. We worked together installing kitchen cabinets for Venture Properties.

"Turn that light off. I can't see a thing," I said.

Crushed cans of Miller Lite had been thrown around when I flipped the truck, so my head was wreathed in dull aluminum. Gravity pulled at my hair, and left me roostered. An empty box of 'Nilla Wafers fell from the door's open panel, and Cedric reached through the shattered windshield to pick up the box and study it.

"I know these things ain't what made you wreck," Cedric said.

"Some deer ran up on me straight out of the woods. You see it?" I asked

He shook his head. "No deer anywhere, just you and the road. You been drinkin', Bud?" He turned and peered down the road.

"Just a little," I said.

"We better hurry and get you out of here before somebody else comes up on us," he told me. "Like the cops. It's a wonder you didn't break your neck."

"You gonna help me out of here? I asked, "my head's bustin'."

"Unbuckle yourself first."

My forehead felt about as swollen as a tick; earlier that summer, I plucked those bloodsuckers out of my beagle's ear with my wife's tweezers. I grabbed a twig out of the front yard and pushed one of the ticks around on the driveway, watching its tiny tick legs fidget. It was too fat to flee. I didn't have the heart to kill it. It was helpless, so I left it there. Sadie sniffed its swollen, gray body, wagged her tail, and then trotted back into the woods where she'd get some more jewelry in her ears.

***

I knew how it felt to not feel full; to not feel like you could ever get your thirst quenched or feel relaxed enough or feel comfortable in your own skin.

My wife, Beth didn't know how bad my drinking had gotten. I thought I had things under control. I thought I could handle myself no matter how much I drank.

I frequented three liquor stores. Visited one every other day, alternating between them in my own little triad of torment so the owners wouldn't think I was a drunk. I still had my rules; still had my values. What mattered was how it looked on the outside.

I'd started to feel a dull pain just below my right ribcage. I thought it was gas at first, but I'd cut pork rinds out of my diet a long time ago. It hurt more when I drank the harder stuff. I knew what it was; nobody had to tell me. I'd go a few days without the drink and that pain would fade away. Then I'd start it all up again when I thought my liver wasn't as aggravated.

Cedric worked me out of the truck, nearly pulling my shoulders out of their sockets.

He left me on my butt and said "I ain't strong enough to pick your big ass up. You gotta stand up on your own."

I touched the bone behind my ear and brought my hand up to my eyes to see if I was bleeding anywhere, but didn't have a single cut on me.

"Your angel's bruised up," he told me.

"What angel?"

"Whichever one just saved your life. I've seen lesser wrecks than this one, and those people didn't survive it."

"It was the deer's fault." I had been driving down the road that night, going just below the speed limit .

"Sure."

"Just what the hell are you doing out this late at night anyways, Ced?"

"About to meet up with up with this girl I'm talkin' to over in Magnolia," said Cedric.

"All those hours throwin' up cabinets together and you didn't tell me you had you a girl?"

"Didn't want to jinx myself," he said.

"You right, you right."

His flashlight flickered and he turned it off. "Thing is almost dead. Come on. I'll drive you over to your house."

I stumbled over an untied shoestring and braced myself on his shoulder.

"How much you drink?" he asked me.

"About half a pint of Old Charter and beer from those cans."

I looked over my shoulder and stared at the warped clothes hanger that held a part of the truck's loose undercarriage together.

"Beth's gonna kill me."

"Come on, man. We done wasted enough time out here."

We got in his truck, and he drove me to my house. He told me that he wished he could stay and help me explain some things to Beth, but Cedric was already running late for his date.

"Let me know how it goes or if you need a place to stay. Call me about picking you up for work on Monday. I can swing by if you need it."

"Okay."

"Hey."

He grabbed my shoulder before I stepped out of the truck.

"Don't do this again, man. I mean it. You're like a brother to me. I know I give you a lot of shit on the job, but you know I'm just teasing you. Don't be going and getting yourself killed. You do it again and I'll stomp a mud hole in you. You hear me?"

"Yeah, I hear you." I nodded and stepped out of the truck. "Let me know how it goes in Magnolia." I shut the door and trudged through the yard to the front porch.

***

When I first started dating Beth, I only drank a glass of wine with her when we went out somewhere nice to eat. Over the three years we'd been married, I started buying a bottle of wine at the end of every other workday and splitting it with her. That turned into Budweiser or Pabst Blue Ribbon every day. I'd volunteer to pick up salad mix and potatoes at the grocery store so that I could mix a six-pack in there without Beth knowing. I'd drink the whole thing before I got home, then collapse the carton and slide it beneath my seat.

Throughout the week, I'd wake up in the middle of the night because I had to take a piss. Then I walked to the kitchen and guzzled water from the sink, but I couldn't go back to sleep— not right then, so I went into the little office we shared. Beth had her sewing machine in there, and I had my old steel guitar that my dad had bought me when I was in high school. I'd pick around on the eight strings, sliding an Ernie Ball bar over the frets, pressing down on the pedals. The knee levers wouldn't work and when I accidently knocked against one of them while playing, they swayed back and forth loosely in their sockets. I imagined Dad sitting there with me, teaching me how to play all over again, telling me how to mute the strings with the fatty part of my hand. In my head, I asked him how he was doing. Dad died a few years back. I didn't get to say goodbye to him and I cried a lot, but eventually drinking and time kept the tears at bay.

The beer wasn't enough, and it made me too bloated so I started stockpiling the hard stuff. That way, I didn't have to drink as much. Beth flipped her lid when she rummaged through my coat closet while I was at work one day. She tore up the place and found two bottles of my good stuff underneath a picture frame with a bunch of winter coats thrown on top and a toolkit thrown on top of those. When I got home from work, I found her standing on the front porch, arms crossed, looking down at the empty glass bottles of Wild Turkey nestled in the grass. She clenched a wet tissue in her hand.

"You poured them out?" I asked.

"That's what you're concerned about?"

"I was saving them for a special occasion." I tapped a finger on my wedding band. "Our three years are comin' up."

"You got the receipts?"

"They didn't give me any."

"That's a lie."

"You know how people are nowadays. They don't like to waste paper."

"This all you bought? How long you been doing this?" She wiped the running mascara from her cheek. "You want me to look through your truck?"

"I just cleaned it out. There's no sense in that."

"I'm sure you did."

"Oh, come on." I told her that she wasn't supposed to be going through my stuff. "That's off limits."

"Thought you weren't hiding this stuff anymore. Not after you let Sadie escape."

"You know what kind of stress I'm under?" I spat in the yard and scratched the tip of my nose.

"You haven't said anything to me about it."

"Boss has been breathing down me and Cedric's necks. We're up to our eyeballs with these new townhomes in Brookhaven that his company's building. Can you imagine how many cabinets we have to install?"

"If you're stressed, why didn't you just tell me?"

***

The night Cedric brought me home from the wreck, I told Beth everything. She told me to pack my bags because she'd had enough.

"I'm gonna call your mom and tell her you need help."

"You can't be airing out my dirty laundry like that. Making something that is supposed to be private so public. Come on, now."

I wrapped my fingers around my belt and twisted the leather until the edges dug into my hip.

"You're not making me a widow." She threw open the screen door and waved me in. "Go on and get your stuff. You can stay at Cedric's place until you get it together."

"Shit almighty, Beth. You can't just go and do all that."

"You think you can stop drinking on your own?" she said as she raised her eyebrows.

"Well, yeah. That's what I said before ain't it?"

"That's what you said before, and now the truck is totaled and you don't have a ride to work."

"So I'll call up Ced, and he'll drive me to work with him. He's cool with that."

"The truck is still gone; the damage is done."

"No, I learned my lesson. I won't drink anymore. I was thinking about it the other day and I'm tired of being tired all the time."

"When we have a kid, you gonna come home and pass out from drinking at work all day? What are you gonna tell our kid? Or are you gonna lie and say you just had a long day at work?"

"I'll be done drinkin by then." I poked the toe of my shoe at a fluffy white filter from one of her cigarettes in the yard.

"That's what you said this summer, but then you also said you needed to drink because of the heat and that only made you angry."

"It was hot."

"You need to start going to AA."

"That's for homeless people."

"You've got to go to some sort of AA meeting somewhere or you're not coming back here."

Our beagle hurried through the open door, bounded off the staircase, and jogged up to me. She whimpered at my feet.

"What about Sadie? She's pregnant," I said. "I need to be here with her when she gives birth so I can help you out."

Sadie stared up at me, wagging her tail and panting hard. I squatted in front of her and rubbed a thumb over the place between her eyes. She squinted and licked her lips. Then she rolled over on her back, her belly full of growing puppies, and I scratched her chest.

"Don't worry about her. She'll be fine."

"But she's mine. I owned her before we got married."

"She's safer here. You're the reason she broke out of her fence and came back pregnant." She clapped her hands and called to the dog, "Sadie, come here."

One day, after my boss got onto me for not making it to a job site on time, I came home and drank away the anger and embarrassment. That night, I forgot to fasten the bungee cord around the broken fence so Sadie wouldn't escape the backyard. The next morning, she was gone and didn't come back for three days. We found out that she was pregnant a month later.

"I can't remember everything."

"Go on and pack up what you need for the week. Then call me when you find a meeting to go to so I know you're okay."

I stood and took out my phone and called Cedric. When he answered, I said "Hey, bud. Guess what?"

***

I found an AA meeting the Thursday after my wreck.

A doorstop was jammed in between two doors at the side of the church, creating a little space. I opened the door, walked through, and went down the stairs.

I shuffled and leaned on a door's push bar to open it. It didn't feel like I was in my body. It didn't feel like I was in control, and there was a far-off ringing in my ears. *I should just turn around*, I thought. I should just sit in the car, listen to some music, and throw away some old fast food trash on the floorboard. I'll tell Beth that I showed up, and they were all weird and no one wanted to talk to me at the end. That's why I didn't stay long and left right after the meeting was over.

I made it through another day not drinking. I'm doing good. I don't need that meeting; I'm not that far gone, I thought.

I walked through a dark hallway where kids met for Sunday school. Tacky display strips lined an unpainted cinder block wall and there were paper characters from the Old Testament sticking to them. Moses' head was a flimsy piece of paper, and he had blue hair and eyebrows. His beard was a bunch of cotton balls, smashed and glued together, and spray-painted gray. One drawing showed a pink whale eating a little man in a robe. Another showed a man sitting in a cave and staring at a bunch of docile lions that were colored lime green. At the far end of the hallway an "Exit" sign burned red. I walked through those double doors, followed the numbers, and as I got close to room 108, the sound of a woman's voice grew louder as she read from a numbered list. The door was open, and I walked right in, threw up a small wave to the few people in there, and sat in a coffee-colored aluminum chair, keeping my eyes on the stained carpet. After the laminated papers were read, the leader of the group asked if it was anyone's first time attending an AA meeting, and his eyes glanced over to me, so I raised my hand.

***

After my fifth meeting in two weeks, a man named Gene came up to me and shook my hand.

"I drank the other day," I told him. "Broke down and bought a sixer."

"How serious are you about all this?" he asked.

"About as serious as I can get."

"Lookin' for a sponsor?"

"Sure. You got room for one more?"

"Come on down with me to the speaker meeting this Friday."

"I don't know that group of people," I whispered.

"You don't have to get up and say anything. Just sit beside me."

"Okay."

"I want you to go up and get your white chip."

"I already got one."

"And you can get another. Since you just had another drink, right?"

"Yeah."

"All right then."

I stared down at the flecked tile. "I don't want to look like a drunk who can't get his act together by getting a second one."

"Ain't no judges there and no one who knows you will be there. Trust me; they'll be glad you came up to get one."

"Okay."

"Remember what the Bible says."

"What's that?" I looked up at him.

"Well, I don't know exactly what it says, but it talks about angels getting all excited over just one person who repents."

"These men ain't angels."

"They get closer to it every day."

"Not me," I said.

"Not yet."

"Yeah."

"I'll pick you up Friday around 5:00 PM. It starts at 6:00 PM, and it's a bit of a drive."

I nodded and pressed the toe of my shoe down on a little rock that had somehow found its way into the building. I moved it toward me, drawing a crooked white line on the linoleum.

"And bring your *Big Book*; like you do when you take your Bible to church."

At AA, I'd been given a book of stories and in it, people talked about what brought them to the point of accepting that their lives were unmanageable because of drinking. I wondered if I was in the same boat they were.

"I haven't seen other people bringing theirs to the meetings. I'm gonna stand out like a sore thumb."

"And that's okay."

"People notice who's new to this whole thing?"

"They do."

"Still embarrassing."

"You'll be with me and it'll be okay." He put his hand on my shoulder.

Beth called my phone a week into my second stint of sobriety and told me to come home.

"Sadie had her babies, and you need to see them. I miss you. Are you okay?"

Later that evening, Cedric dropped me off at the house.

When I stepped inside, I saw six puppies snuggled up to their momma on an old comforter that Beth and I used to share. They were at the foot of the couch in the living room and I crouched a few feet away from them to watch them sleep. Sadie looked like she was suffocated by their tiny breathing bodies. When she saw me, she lifted her head, then dropped it back down and closed her eyes.

Beth came up from behind me and put her hand on my shoulder. She squatted next to me, watching the sleeping litter of beagles.

"There was a man at the group the other night," I said. "He talked about his story and I related to it. Is that weird?"

"The AA group? What'd he say?"

"Talked about the warm feeling that came over him when he used to drink and as more that feeling comes on, it feels like a hug. So he drank more and more, until he did stuff he couldn't remember. That warm feeling he talked about is why I drink too."

"But you have me to hug you." She traced my shoulder blade with her fingernails.

"I know."

"Is that not good enough? Am I not good enough?"

"Yeah it is, and you are."

She nodded.

"I grew up on the football fields, baseball fields, and basketball courts." I rubbed a thumb against my wedding band. "You know one time when I was in the fourth grade, I was playing Pop Warner football and I caught an interception. I never thought I'd be able to catch the ball because all I ever played was defense, and those quarterbacks either overthrew all of us or came up short, but this time the ball barely got over the line of scrimmage. It was tipped off a lineman's fingers, and it wobbled through the air. I played middle linebacker back then, and I caught it. Did I ever tell you that?"

"No, but it doesn't surprise me."

"I ran it all the way back and scored."

"Well, look at you," she said.

"You know what my dad did after the game was over and our team won?"

"What?"

"He dragged one of those big-ass coolers, with the little wheels in the back, out into the end zone. I can still see him dragging it out there in his red muscle shirt and Reebok shoes. He opened the lid and started tossing cans of root beer to the team. Then, he hustled over to me and picked me up right there in my sweaty uniform and pads. He picked me up with such force that I dropped my helmet."

"He was strong. I remember seeing pictures of him. Didn't he win some kind of strongman competition?"

"Yeah he did. That day on the football field, he told me that he loved me and he kissed me on my ear. I got a little embarrassed, but then I felt like I was king of the world. In my dad's arms, I could see over everything and everybody."

"I'm glad you have that memory," she said.

"I want him to hug me again. I want him to hug me and pick me up and tell me that everything's gonna be okay, and that he's proud of me. I want him to be here right now. If I could snap my fingers and bring him back, I would."

"And you know what he'd say?"

"No."

"That he can't come back," she whispered. "He doesn't want to come back because he's made it to the best place there is, and no one wants to come back from that. Not if you've been there."

"Yeah." I bit my bottom lip.

"But he'd also tell you that you're as strong as he was, if not, stronger. You have his hands and his heart and his smile. That's what he gave you, and he's never gonna leave you."

"I'd tell him that I was sorry for making things so hard on him, and for making him spend money on things that I broke around the house when money was so hard to come by back then."

"Look at me." She grabbed my chin and turned my head toward her.

I looked her in the eyes, and then looked down at the veins in my hand.

"None of that matters. You have to move forward, because that's what he'd want you to do," she said.

"I'm sorry for putting you through all this crap with my drinking."

She leaned in and wrapped her arms around me.

"You're still that guy who carried two waffle cones full of double-scoop chocolate ice cream over to me on our first date, and I can still imagine you looking down at those cones."

"I didn't want them to melt off."

"I wouldn't have cared," she said.

"I want to make things right."

"Then run it all the way back like you did on that field; back to who you used to be and back to the man I married."

I wrenched my wallet out of my back pocket, opened it, and took out an old picture of myself in third grade and showed it to her.

"Look at this."

"Why do you have that?"

"I've been carrying it with me ever since Dad died."

She took it from me and studied it.

"Look at that gap-toothed smile. That's a real smile right there."

"I don't smile like that anymore."

"I saw you smile like that on our wedding day when I was walking down the aisle."

"Really?"

"You don't remember?"

"I was pretty nervous that day."

She stuck her finger in my chest.

"It's still in there."

I pulled her to me, held her tight, and kissed the top of her head. Then I looked at the fireplace mantel and saw a framed picture of Dad smiling and holding me in his big arms right after I was born.

I closed my eyes.

I didn't want to let go.

Spring

JAMES HARTMAN

They are sitting on the patio outside their apartment, the sun a dirty glow behind a dark paste of cloud.

"Everything will die, Tom," his wife says. "It might not seem that way because it's been unusually warm, but the cold always returns, and when it does everything dies."

"Why don't you want to know why, Sandra?" he asks.

"You can see the flowers already blooming." She points at the row of flowers in their yard. "They're so bright and happy and alive. Little do they know they're about to die."

"You know what I mean, Sandra," he says, not looking at the row of flowers. "Don't you want to know why I'm divorcing you?"

"It doesn't matter why. It won't change anything."

"I want to explain," he says. "I need to explain." He closes his eyes.

"Before I started interacting with girls, I was even-keeled. I didn't think I was great or handsome, but neither did I think I was horrible or ugly. I was just okay. Maybe I made really poor choices in the girls I dated, I don't know, but the girls I chose were constantly belittling me. They were always ogling other guys and blabbering about them, just shoving them in my face. My first serious girlfriend and I were going to a movie and she saw this poster of an actor outside the theatre and she looked me right in my eye and said, 'Why can't you have arms like that?' That was the beginning. Every single one of my girlfriends did these kinds of things, but some were worse than others."

Sandra shifts in her chair, and starts spinning her thumbs. Tom squeezes his eyes, hard.

"The very worst I experienced was when we first met. I mean, you couldn't watch a fucking commercial without saying something about the guy in it. Do you know what that does when it happens multiple times a day, every single day?"

Sandra stops shifting and she stops spinning her thumbs.

"You can't help but start thinking," Tom says, opening his eyes, "That maybe everyone's right, and maybe there's a good reason why everyone belittles me. Maybe I *am* worthless and ugly. After so many years of girl after girl doing the same thing, maybe they *are* right, or why else would they do it? Why would someone talk so obsessively to their partner, whom they supposedly love, about being so attracted to someone else? I mean, I was all over you, Sandra. I told you I loved your long red hair; I told you I loved it when you cut it short because it looked great both ways. I told you I loved your body and found it attractive even when you thought your thighs and hips were getting too big. So, why would I ever talk so obsessively about being attracted to some girl who appears on a goddamn television screen? I think if someone obsesses over someone like that then maybe they should find a way to tell that person how they feel, because it's like they're unhappy or unsatisfied with what they have. What is so wrong and horrible about obsessing over the person you're with? I told you how all that made me feel and you promised you would change, but then your eyes would flash on someone and I knew what you were feeling because your neck would get red and your body would get hot and I knew you were still desiring other men; like you just couldn't help it. Maybe some women are just programmed that way." Tom's heart was racing. "And so when I met a woman who *didn't* do any of these things to me, who obsessed over *me*, I guess it didn't matter that I had a ring on my finger."

Sandra does not shift in her chair, and she doesn't spin her thumbs. She doesn't do anything except close her eyes, briefly. Perhaps she is merely squinting, as if somewhere beyond the row of blooming flowers there is a blueprint for how she can respond.

"I've been seeing her for three months, and you know what?"

This part he told himself he wouldn't say, but he can't help it.

"I don't feel an ounce of shame. For the first time in my life I am free, not weighted down by fear of what might be said any second that will make me feel less about myself." Tom continues, but he does not say that her name is Jenny, or that he met her at the bookstore on the intracoastal waterway, or that she's five foot, two inches tall and her right leg is an inch shorter than her left, or that every time he sees her rub her right knee she's so self-conscious about it he can't help but fall more in love with her.

Sandra's eyes shut, completely, and her eyelids ripple, as if she is searching inside them for something she could not find out here.

"Do you know why everything will eventually die, Tom? It is because the flowers are too vulnerable. All that sunlight and warmth arrived before it should have and everything bloomed too soon, and because everything has bloomed too soon everything will now die. The cold will come blowing back and kill every single thing." She scrunched her eyes.

"If what you're saying is that we got married too young, Sandra, you'd be wrong. The truth is that I never should have married you in the first place.

As Tom watched the dark clouds part the feeling of the warm sun seeped through them.

The truth," Tom says, "is that everything has a way of blooming right on time."

David Drake

RICHARD NICKEL

The story of David Drake. Born a slave and learned to make pottery and wrote poems on his pottery during a time when it was illegal to do so. He saw the end of the Civil War and gained his freedom. His pottery is highly treasured and is now in museum collections.

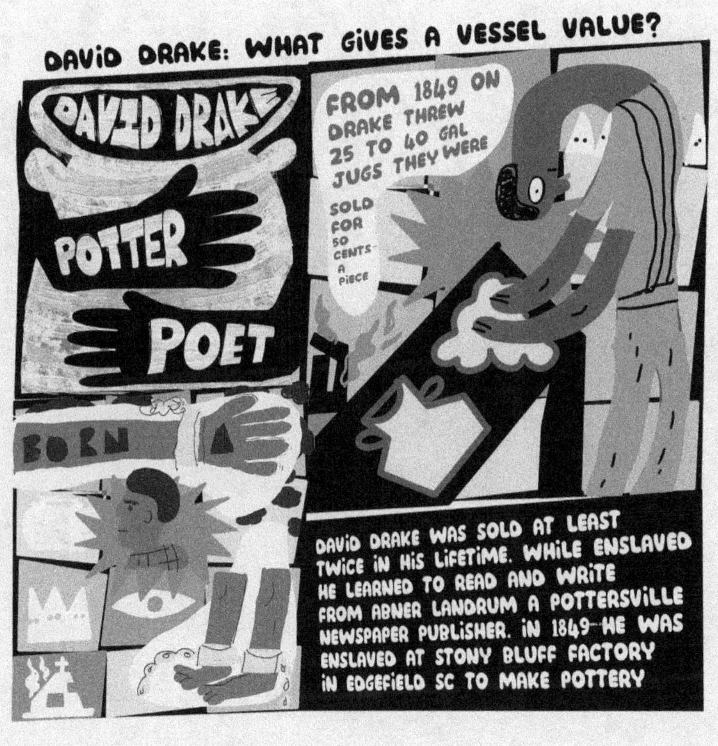

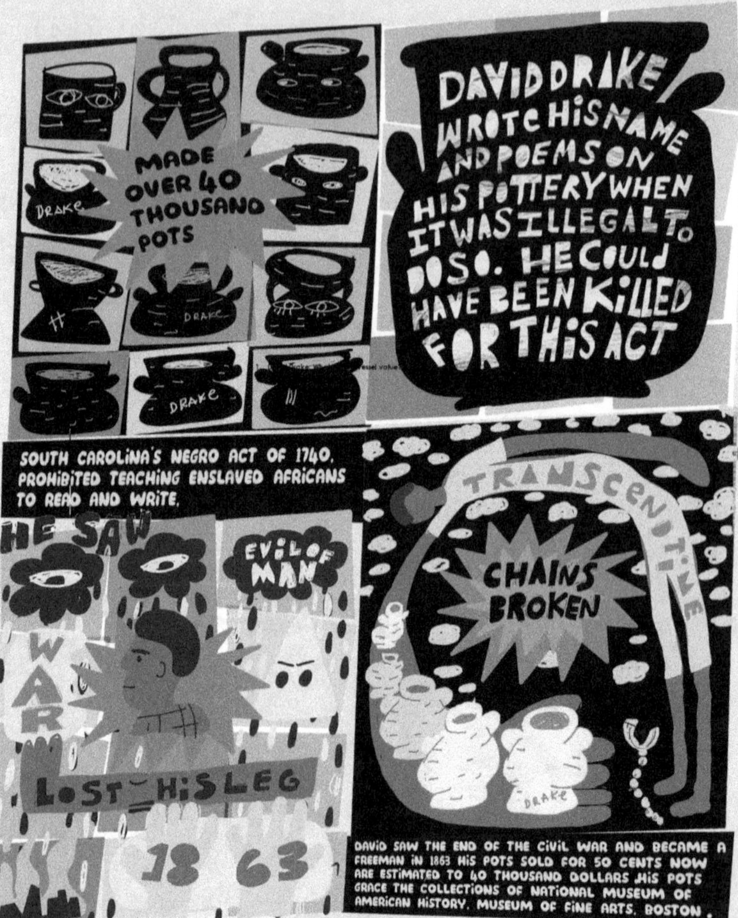

MADE OVER 40 THOUSAND POTS
DRAKE
DRAKE
DRAKE
DAVID DRAKE WROTE HIS NAME AND POEMS ON HIS POTTERY WHEN IT WAS ILLEGAL TO DO SO. HE COULD HAVE BEEN KILLED FOR THIS ACT
SOUTH CAROLINA'S NEGRO ACT OF 1740, PROHIBITED TEACHING ENSLAVED AFRICANS TO READ AND WRITE.
HE SAW
EVIL OF MAN
WAR
LOST HIS LEG
18 63
TRANSCENDING
CHAINS BROKEN
DRAKE
DAVID SAW THE END OF THE CIVIL WAR AND BECAME A FREEMAN IN 1863 HIS POTS SOLD FOR 50 CENTS NOW ARE ESTIMATED TO 40 THOUSAND DOLLARS HIS POTS GRACE THE COLLECTIONS OF NATIONAL MUSEUM OF AMERICAN HISTORY, MUSEUM OF FINE ARTS, BOSTON.

The Line: A Play in One Act

ETHAN CUNNINGHAM

(in the style of Harold Pinter)

TIME: Unknown.

PLACE: An empty stage.

CHARACTERS: Duncan, Milkmaid, Tall Man, Young Woman, Youth, Guard, & Others *been given a letter of direction. A GUARD stands just SL of the line's end. He is a large man with big arms crossed in front of him, while his face bears a stern look. Behind him is a two-wheel handcart upon which is a smooth stone slab.*

A small man, DUNCON, enters wearing a cap and carrying his letter of direction in front of him, checking it to make sure he has arrived at the proper place. He looks around curiously, but almost bewildered. He fully turns around, examines the sign, the letter, the line, and the person at the rear of the line. He stands on his toes trying to see where the line goes, but it is no use. The line advances one body. This takes DUNCON by surprise. He re-examines the line again. The GUARD comes forward and grabs DUNCON, putting him in the last place in line. DUNCON is again bewildered.>

DUNCON

What's all this then?

GUARD

<Sternly.>

Get in line.

<DUNCON, pleaded to the others.>

DUNCON

You can't treat me this way. They can't treat me this way! Let go!

<Now that DUNCON is in his spot, the GUARD returns to his position. DUNCON looks at the people

and their apparent ignorance of his plight, then at the
GUARD *who seems to lack all recognition of his exis-*
tence.>

What's all this then?

    <He looks around some more.>

I hope this is the place. This is the place. The place in the letter.

    <To a large MILKMAID *in front of him, carrying a*
    metal milk jug and a letter sticking partially out of her
    breast. She is middle-aged and well-built. DUNCON *is*
    dwarfed by her. DUNCON *shows her the letter.>*

I got a letter. Directs me to this exact location. A letter, right here. Says, 'To whom it may concern, preferably Mr. Duncon Gert. Have sent a letter with directions, please proceed to the point as designated by the diagram A...

    <He shows the splayed letter to the MILKMAID, *who*
    glances but otherwise takes little notice.>

...and take your place in the line.' Now you see, I'm here—with the letter. And I've found it. The line. I've found the line.

    <Pause. No one is paying him heed.>

The letter said go to the line. I went to the line, I'm in the line.

    <Pause.>

Am I in the right line? The line? I know the sign over there says it is, a line anyway, whether it's the right one or not though. I could be in the wrong line.

<*Pause.* DUNCON *looks around.*>

S'pose I'm early then.

<*The line advances one body. Everyone shuffles forward except for* DUNCON, *who is distancing himself in preparation to leave SL.*>

This can't be right. It's got to be the wrong line. I'm leaving. Leaving then.

<DUNCON *turns to go, only to be stopped by the* GUARD.>

GUARD
<*As intimidating as possible.*>

Get back in line.

DUNCON

But it's not the right line.

GUARD

Get. Back. In. Line.

<DUNCON *saunters back to his place, eye-checking the* GUARD, *who stands firm until* DUNCON *is in his proper place. The* GUARD *resumes his regular position.*>

DUNCON

It's not the right line. I'm sure it's not.

<He looks about, curious.>

Everyone's so...old. Don't tell me I'm the youngest fellow here!

> *<The* MILKMAID *looks back at him for a moment before returning.* DUNCON *removes his cap and scrunches it in his hands as he approaches the* MILK-MAID *from the DSL side.>*

Tell me, mum, what're you in for? Not really sure what I'm in for. No one's ever sure what they're in for, what they're getting into, until they've done it. Till they've got there. Only it's not such a drab place.

> *<Looking around, mentioning things as he examines them.>*

Colorful people. A sign. A cart. Earth, ground. Lovely, lovely ground. And a man, or a guard, or gardener, or shepherd. Maybe a shepherd.

<To the MILKMAID.*>*

What do you think he is? A shepherd?

<Pause as he thinks.>

No staff. Shepherds have staffs, I think. Big hook on the end. And sheep. And woolen clothes, he's got woolen clothes. At least I think they're woolen clothes. Too hard to tell from here, and if I take a step out of line that lug'll wipe my face with those ham-hock hands of his. But what a face he's got. By the looks of him I'd think he was bricklayer, or by the arms a blacksmith. Or with all that, rotundness, a butcher. A butcher, he looks like a butcher.

<To the MILKMAID.>

Doesn't he look like a butcher?

<She shakes her head "no.">

Oh. Not a butcher.

<Pause.>

No apron. Clever girl. No apron. You've got to have an apron if you're a butcher. Experience. Experience. You've got an apron, he doesn't. You would know. You would know.

> <Pause. He tries to ask the MILKMAID another question.>

Do you think—?

> <The line advances one body without DUNCON. He notices the gap between him and the MILKMAID, but does not close it.>

GUARD

Line!

> <DUNCON realizes the problem and hops into the next spot. A new person enters from SL: a TALL MAN, younger than the MILKMAID or DUNCON. He carries a ratty satchel with a strange symbol on it.>

DUNCON

Who's that then? Who are you?

> *<Without paying* DUNCON *any heed whatsoever, the* TALL MAN *proceeds to take his place in line behind* DUNCON. DUNCON's *diminutive stature is thrown into stark contrast now that he's sandwiched between the* MILKMAID *and the* TALL MAN.>*

Whew! Close.

> *<Turning his attention to* TALL MAN.>*

Feel a bit stuffy to you?

> *<The* TALL MAN *looks down at him for a moment before looking straight ahead once more.>*

No? Not stuffy. Easy being tall isn't it? Don't have to breathe off everyone's chest. Lucky you.

> *<*DUNCON *crosses his arms and turns to face straight ahead.>*

Being a person of small stature isn't easy. As a man, no less.

> *<He looks back and notices that the* TALL MAN *still stares straight ahead.>*

What is it everyone's looking at anyway? Can't see a thing like this. Small stature. Not large in the vertical—or horizontal. It's a vice, I'll be sworn. If there's any virtue to be had in such minute features, I'd be the first to know. Been small all my life. That's why I joined the service. You ever in the service? Arms and a chest like that...should be in the service, if you're not already. Old big arms over there is in the service. Least, I think he is. Probably not. Too fat. Makes me wonder, you know. Why we're all here, this motley, all peasant folk. And he's over there. Doesn't make much sense really. Nothing makes much sense really. Take this line for instance. Here we are, standing in line, you all looking straight ahead at something I can't see. And he's over there. I mean, we're just standing. Oh every now and then it moves, the line that is, but not often. Not often. Not regular enough for it to matter. For all I know we could be standing here all day. Maybe all night.

<He squints, looking up into the sky.>

Weather. Can't tell what time of day it is. Enough light for day. Could be a bright night. Moon and all. No moon, though. No sun. Stars are hiding.

<He notices the symbol on the TALL MAN's satchel.>

Ahh! You are in the service! I knew it, I knew it, I did! The service! Only...that's not any rank I know. What rank is that?

<No response from the TALL MAN, so DUNCON turns to the MILKMAID.>

What rank you suppose that is?

<Pause. DUNCON's mouth hangs open. She ignores him.>

You don't know nothing about rank.

<DUNCON *looks back to the* TALL MAN.>

If you were in the service, you'd know a thing or two about rank. 'Sides if a man's worth marrying.

<*He turns to face the* TALL MAN. DUNCON *scratches his head.*>

Still... funny rank, that. If it is a rank. Unless...you're not from around here, are you? Probably not. Not with a face like that.

<DUNCON *turns back the other way.*>

A bit young if you ask me. More youth than I've got anyway.

<*Pause. He observes the line for a bit and then faces the* TALL MAN *again.*>

It's strange, but I think...the oldest folk are at the front of the line, aren't they? And youngest folk...why...I think you're the youngest man here. I'm not exactly silver-headed yet, either. Maybe—

<*The line advances another body. The* TALL MAN *gives* DUNCON *a strange, menacing look.* DUNCON *looks back to see the line has moved.*>

Oh.

<DUNCON *quickly gets to his new place. Pause. He bounces on the balls of his feet. He looks back at the* TALL MAN, *at his bag, at the symbol, and then double-takes. He turns to the* TALL MAN *and bends over to examine the strange symbol more closely.*>

Does that say...? No, no I guess not. What *does* it say? It's rather worn, don't you think? Not a talkative chap, are you? No. Not talkative. It's funny what this says. Listen to this, it says, "Doncun e useus nom kenov." Only they've spelled my name wrong. It's Duncon, D-U-N-C-O-N, not D-O-N-C-U-N. You see, they've reversed the vowels. It's all muddled. My name. Why you think they'd muddle up my name for no good purpose? It's the only name I've got, no sense in muddling it up. And where's everyone else's names? They got a badge, too? What's it mean, then?

I mean, it's got to mean something. Can't be nothing. Nothing can't mean nothing. Even nothing means something. When you ask a bloke what's wrong, and he says, nothing, that means something. Oldest trick in the brain. Say nothing when you mean something. Some people are different though. Oh yeah. Different. They say a lot, when they actually mean nothing. All words, no deeds.

<Pause.>

Why you think that is then? Always talking, never listening. Sad really. Poor blokes don't value the truth of silence. What we can't say with our lips, we can say with our silence.

<Pause.>

Forget who said that.

<Pause.>

Huh. Only it's funny, see, 'cause you can't say nothing by saying something. 'Cause even nothing means something. Take that for instance. That nonsense there. "Doncun e useus nom kenov." Bit of rubbish, isn't it?

<Pause. DUNCON *waits to see if the* TALL MAN *will ever respond.>*

Silent type, eh? Psh. You know, you and her would be a good match for each other. Eh? Eh? Very good. Both the silent folk. Not much for words, no. Not at all. A perfect match see. She probably likes the large, silent type. At least, I think she does. Then again, I really don't know. Can't remember. Did she…?

*<*DUNCON *finally notices the* YOUNG WOMAN.*>*

What's this? Hold on. Hold on. What's this?

<Wide-eyed, he X DSL to the YOUNG WOMAN, *pointing to her with his hat. He asks the* TALL MAN *who turns to see what he is talking about.>*

Who you think this is?

<The TALL MAN *turns back to face forward once more.>*

Hello hello.

GUARD

Line!

DUNCON

Hold on, hold on, I've got an inspection to make.

GUARD

> *<More adamant as he X to DUNCON and grabs him, pulling him back to his place.>*

Line! Stay! In! Line!

> *<Pause as DUNCON recomposes himself. He scowls at the GUARD as he returns to his regular position.>*

DUNCON

It's not a very good line.

> *<Pause. He ruminates. He glances at the MILK-MAID, the TALL MAN, attempts to look back at the YOUNG WOMAN without getting out of line, and then back to the TALL MAN.>*

It's getting shorter.

> *<Back to the TALL MAN.>*

The line. The front of the line. It's getting shorter. I think we're almost there. All this waiting and we're almost there. It's been a long line. Don't know why. Don't even know what we're waiting for.

> *<Pause. DUNCON looks around back to the TALL MAN.>*

Do you know what we're waiting for? I mean, we've been standing here for half an hour, at least I think it's been half an hour. Feels like ten hours if it's been a half, you know what I mean? Worse than Sundays it is. Is today Sunday? No? No, no one knows. Can't even tell what bloody time of day it is. Or night. How can no one know what day it is! No one knows nothing around here. All deaf and dumb everyone is. Not worth a penny to speak a thought since it all comes to no ears. Words without purpose, that's what they are. Words without cause.

<Pause. DUNCON *tries to see what lies ahead.>*

What you suppose happens? When we get there. When we get to the end of the line. What happens? Is it a prize? Could be cake. Could be tea.

<Pause.>

Could be more of you blokes. More lines.

<Pause.>

Could be a firing squad.

<Pause.>

Think it's something good?

<He prods the TALL MAN *with his hat. The* TALL MAN *notices.>*

You think they'll feed us?

TALL MAN

I'pische.

> <The TALL MAN *resumes his robotic stare forward.*
> *Pause.* DUNCON *is stunned.*>

DUNCON

"Ipeesh?" What does that mean? Hey. What does "ipeesh" mean?

> <Silence.>

Fine bloke you are. Not much of a friend. Though I suppose we were never really friends anyway. More like acquaintances. Hard to make friends when you're the only one talking and no one's listening.

> <The line advances once more leaving only the
> MILKMAID *in front of* DUNCON. *He voices his ex-*
> *citement to the* TALL MAN *as they both shuffle for-*
> *ward.*>

Look at that, the line's moving again. Just one more. One more. 'Till we get to...'ipeesh.' Or, wherever it is. Could be just the other side of that wall. Could be. Just the wall. Lot of wait just to see the other side of that wall.

> <Pause. He nods to himself.>

What you suppose is over there? Another wall? Could be another line. Bet you it is. You watch, we'll get to the end of this line, and next thing you know we're at the beginning of another. Don't think my knees can take another queue. Rather senseless don't you think? All these lines, put up back to back. Facing each other. Some got rifles. Others—they don't. Makes you think. Gets the brain working. I wonder...

<Pause.>

Maybe at the end of this line, there are no more lines. Maybe there's nothing. Maybe a tribunal. A court. Maybe we'll be tried for every minute detail of our lives.

<He laughs.>

Imagine that! Everything we ever done, watched and criticized by some old pervert in a beard. Psh.

<Pause. A new person enters from SL to fill the line. It is a YOUTH, *the youngest yet.* DUNCON *watches as the* YOUTH *fills the rear position.>*

Or maybe I'm dreaming. And the only reason none of you talk is 'cause I can't think of nothing for you all to say. Except "ipeesh." I don't know what that is. Sounds like a sneezing peach, only I haven't eaten no peaches or sneezed lately. And what's this with lines? You'd think a line would lead somewhere. Only, it doesn't. Or maybe this line leads somewhere...and I just can't see it. Itches my skin when I can't see what's ahead. Hard to concentrate on enjoying the journey, know what I mean?

<Pause. He prods the MILKMAID *with his hat.>*

What's up there, then? What can you see? Is it pasture? A room? A man? A woman? A thing?

<Pause. She looks at him but says nothing.>

Oh, come on! Ipeesh!

Hey you! Yeah! You, fat man! Who the fuck are you! What's that for, eh? That for carrying off our things? I got a letter. A fucking letter. That's why I'm here. That's why all of us are here! We. Got. Fucking. Letters. Orders. Commands. You going to carve our names into that stone there? With what? Your fucking fat fingers? I'll tell you what you can do with that sign...

Why the sign...? Hey. Fat fingers. What's with the sign? Why doesn't it tell us where we're going, and not just where to go? Following blind orders—I've done that. I'm done with it. Didn't have much here in this line. I'm done with the service and that means I'm done with orders. Just a bloke now. Nothing special. I do my letters. Got one here.

Right here. Yeah. My fucking letter! Don't suppose you've got a letter, then?

We've all got letters. We're all in line, but him. There's a sign. A man. A cart. And a flat rock.

And the line.

> *<Pause.>*

Why the fucking line!

> *<The line advances one more body. DUNCON hesitantly shuffles forward to the front. No one is ahead of him. Pause. He breathes heavily and tries to walk away, X DSL.>*

Can't do this. Can't do this.

GUARD

Line!

> *<The TALL MAN grabs DUNCON by the arm and yanks him back into place. DUNCON is stunned. He stares at the TALL MAN, then at the ground, at the GUARD, and back to the TALL MAN.>*

DUNCON

Ipeesh, eh? Ipeesh?

> *<Pause. He looks up, seeing that it's his turn to exit SR. A YOUNG BOY no older than 12 enters from SL to fill the last slot in the line.>*

GUARD

Line!

DUNCON

No, no.

GUARD

<More forceful.>

Line!

DUNCON

No, it's a –

GUARD

<Even more forceful.>

Line! Advance! Line!

DUNCON

No fucking way!

<DUNCON X to SL as the GUARD comes out to meet him.>

GUARD

Liiiiiine!

<The GUARD knocks DUNCON flat with his fists. He pulls an old pistol and points it at DUNCON's face.>

Line.

<DUNCON slowly X back to his place at the front of the line, walking backwards while the GUARD remains pointing the pistol at DUNCON's face from the same distance. They maintain eye contact.>

Line, advance.

<DUNCON *looks back to his destination off SR and then back down the barrel of the pistol.*>

Line. Advance.

<DUNCON *gulps. He finally shuffles off, exiting SR. The line advances to fill his position. The* GUARD *returns to his regular position and puts the gun away. Long Pause. From SL enters a* YOUNG BOY, *dressed exactly like* DUNCON, *his features reminiscent of* DUNCON *as well. The* YOUNG BOY *carries his letter in front of him, checking it to make sure he's arrived at the proper place, but it is obvious that he cannot yet read. He looks around, examining the sign, the letter, the line, and the person at the back of the line. He stands on his toes trying to see where the line goes, but it is no use. He re-examines the line again.*>

YOUNG BOY

What's all this, then?

GUARD

<*Sternly.*>

Get in line.

<*The* YOUNG BOY *reacts to the guard. He looks back at his letter and then at the line. He's overwhelmed. His mouth is open, just about to speak when—BLACKOUT. CURTAIN. END OF PLAY.*>

Three Paintings by Edward Hopper

LAURA BONAZZOLI

I. Automat

Listen. It's okay.
No words needed.
The raw umber night moans,
the pewter bulbs blare,
but I hear
the muted chirp
of your cadmium yellow hat,
your cheeks' vermilion cry,
your velvet coat viridian
sotto voce
-like divulging
your creamy flesh,
one gloveless hand warmed
by your cobalt turquoise cup.
Don't look up.

No restrained recounting
of your dreams required,
how you lost
your glove or who

it was that used to sit across
a pool of pale cerulean
table speaking,
speaking while you watched
your coffee cooling
in your cup, and tasted
too much sugar
in your permanent rose mouth.

II. Room in Brooklyn

She said, Not today,
Josephine,
not today.
She said, Take
these roses but the world's
not ready for us yet.
Wait.
Don't ever tire
of waiting, watch
everything that waits
with you there, across
this city from the window
where I sit and wait
to part
your blue gown.

III. Hotel Window

Economy excuses nothing.
One chooses.
To pin one's brightest hat, for instance,
at a slant upon one's sturdy curls,
above a post-war dress and fling
one's pre-war coat (no matter,
mink will always be in season)
over stalwart shoulders, blue
lining flowing like the sea,
and seat oneself erect
upon a tawdry plank of sofa
as if on a royal barge
and gaze out like a duchess
or the consort of a king.

One chooses such defiance—
one might even say theatrics—
that the bellhop or the desk clerk
might suppose one waits for someone
human—grandson, lover, lawyer—
not a yellow taxi to transport one further,
ever further from the last
mementos of one's careful,
squandered life.

nightmares that formed me

SARA GILBERT

today, i saw KKK hoods at walmart.
they didn't look at me twice, because
the outside of me fits with their vision
of white and blonde and blue-eyed but

when i was four, we moved to central florida
and i was told not to mention chanukah,
yiddish, not repeat the word mishpacha,
mumble beginnings of jewish prayers—
mom and dad said bad people would hurt us.

we moved again when i was nine—i
knew not to mention catholicism either,
no prayers to saint mary, to call myself
"christian." every night we looked

for crosses burning. we sat waiting
for painted swastikas on our
garage door, people to yell
what we knew: we didn't belong.
i didn't tell anyone i grew up in a

mixed religion home until
seventeen, when no one would
call us heebs or shylocks, once
i could explain how both

these beliefs raised me, formed
me, made me. i didn't fall
into the perfectly marked
boxes of "jew" or "catholic."

even at the age of thirty, i'm
scared of people burning crosses,
ones who spray paint nazi symbols
they're still in my nightmares—

i'm seven years old, watching
wood and grass go up in flames.

Backpacking

JILL BRONFMAN

Dylan had twenty-three hours left
Of the twenty-four he had agreed
To be left alone in the near desert
Of the last-chance mountains

He had already twisted two lanyards
Around his left wrist
Drawn four lizards in all, not moving
(except for their trippy necks)
And turned them into monsters.

No wait, he could still
Smooth the sleeping bag out from its roll
Pour water into his canteen and sip
Stare at the clouds

Dylan had never been alone before
This moment
Waiting in line by himself
Used to count, a solo cup
Did not count now, no more would count
A bee kept him company, for a few seconds
A rock stayed longer, was up for a chat

The sun leaned down to embrace the hills
And the young man laid back to observe
Not the sunset, as he had expected,
But the whole sky.

Haughty

TERRY SAVOIE

If there had been one word for her
back then, it would have been "haughty"
with those lush tresses hanging down
so that they nearly reached
Mother Earth as she bent over,
her hair slightly swaying in the wind.

O, she knew very well what she had & how
her admirers valued what it was as they
passed by & saw her each morning.

Yes, *haughty* would be the one word
I'd choose since she took her
looks so very seriously, but when
those groomers came in to trim her,
well, after that, she simply appeared forlorn.

But that's been better for four years now,
& she's coming around again, shaking
those new mid-length tresses,
what she's grown since
having being so rudely shorn,
shaking her new growth in the breezes.

Not that much are they, I know, although
they're better by far than what they've been.
Dog walkers go by, smile & comment on
how happy she seems to be doing of late.

That's how it is with my paper birch
as I'm beginning to watch her nod
in recognition & breathe so
much more easily with
each passing season.

Road Map

RICK CHRISTMAN

A mossy oak stands alone
Across the lane from my house,
A trunk broad enough
To house Merlin,
The limbs stretch tall and wide,
Like gathering arms
Along the drainage pond,
As if the tree guards the place.

Sometimes, on a starry night,
I watch the moss wave, shimmer,
As if the tree whispers,
Moves in rhythm
With inspired breath and words
Of a thousand mouths.

Sometimes, in the daylight,
I trace the oak's
Dark interior branches,
As they wind and swirl and twist,
Like a road map
Giving directions to a place
More important
Than where I am.

But the mossy oak
Also bears the relentless Southern Sun,
Bears vicious, whipping
Hurricane winds and rain,
Bending its creaking top branches down
And back up,
Like bowing to an unknown audience.

Now I watch the
Oak bend nearly to breaking,
The moss sweeping the ground
Over and over,
Until the winds cease.
Then rights itself
As if it never faltered.

Fishermen

STEVEN DEUTSCH

I don't believe
I've been this
way before.

The trail
narrowing
and narrowing

again,
has become
little more

than a scratch
in the undergrowth.
But I am not lost—

I can
smell the scent
of water ahead

and there, just
around the bend—
Spring Creek.

We fished
this spot
one summer

years ago
vowing to become
fly fishermen.

"Trout on the grill,"
you'd shout
with your usual

enthusiasm,
"I can hear
them sizzle."

But that last
summer of childhood
we learned more

of the feeding habits
of the North American mosquito
than of rainbow trout.

It was so much fun—
I thought
with a smile

I sent your way—
to wherever it may be
that you have landed.

American Songs

FRANK DULLAGHAN

June 2020

My first time in New York, I stood on top
of one of the Twin Towers and looked down the length
of Manhattan towards the Empire State Building:
a different country, a different time.
I was nostalgic for places whose names I'd picked up from songs –
Here, high, in New York, New York, I was the only living boy.
But I also, wanted to be shown the way to San Bernardino,
Alabama's sweet home, the deep heart of Texas.
Georgia was on my mind, Indiana wanted me –
names that were shrines to grandeur and adventure.

Perhaps it's just that I've grown up, have been disappointed
by life enough times for the luster to have dulled.
Perhaps it's just that I have become more aware
of the brutish, ignorant, racist, undercurrents; the ugliness
of so many suited politicians. It's not even that the place names
have lost their magic, it's that the magic has been stolen,
the potential for wonder squandered.

How can I go back now? America is an old liner
travelling further and further out to sea, losing sight
of land, friends, past. An epidemic rages and the captain

won't take the helm. The ship is in flames, police practice
their murderous arts on the deck, in the gangways;
the crew have neglected their sworn duty and would arm
all the crazies in the name of freedom. I could not visit again
when it's like this. Goodbye Galveston. Don't hold that midnight train
to Georgia, I won't be on it. Don't show me the way to San Jose.
I am heartbroken. It's not even my country and I my heart is broken.
Woodstock was a long time ago.

Pine Cones

JACK STEWART

for Vivian

1.
Wooden petals that spread enough
To catch snow, white-tipped tufts
Stiffened by frost—seeds long gone
To birds the size of cones
Themselves, waxwings, nuthatches,
The finches that twitch
In gusts. In the Song of Songs,
The face of her beloved is young
And "excellent as the cedars,"
Though he abandoned her.
These shelter the easily
Harvested, the chickadees
Like small fists of snow, the sparrows
That twist like dead leaves
Caught in the needles. Branch-ends sieve
The light sparingly.
Harder than dried ears of corn,
These dark, tapered cones
Embedded in the cold,
The future windfalls of the cold—

2.

For a Christmas centerpiece,
My daughter fills a bowl
With pine cones and sprigs of holly,
The dark green, barb-edged,
Reflecting the candlelight.
Red berries of wax
Melting down those stems.
She soaked the cones for half an hour,
Then dried them under a hot lamp.
She collected them under field-edge pines,
Not in a bag at a nursery,
Wanting ones that had known the cold
And cloudless nights,
Or at least the cold she'd felt,
The nights she'd shouldered under.
Only then could she be sure
They would be ready for celebration,
Ready to curve through shorter days.
And in a few weeks tossed on the fire
To burn down to purest ash
She'll mix with soil for the Chinese evergreens,
The bromeliads and potted ferns
To start the new year.

AI News

PATRICK MCEVOY

short graphic story illustrated in 2015

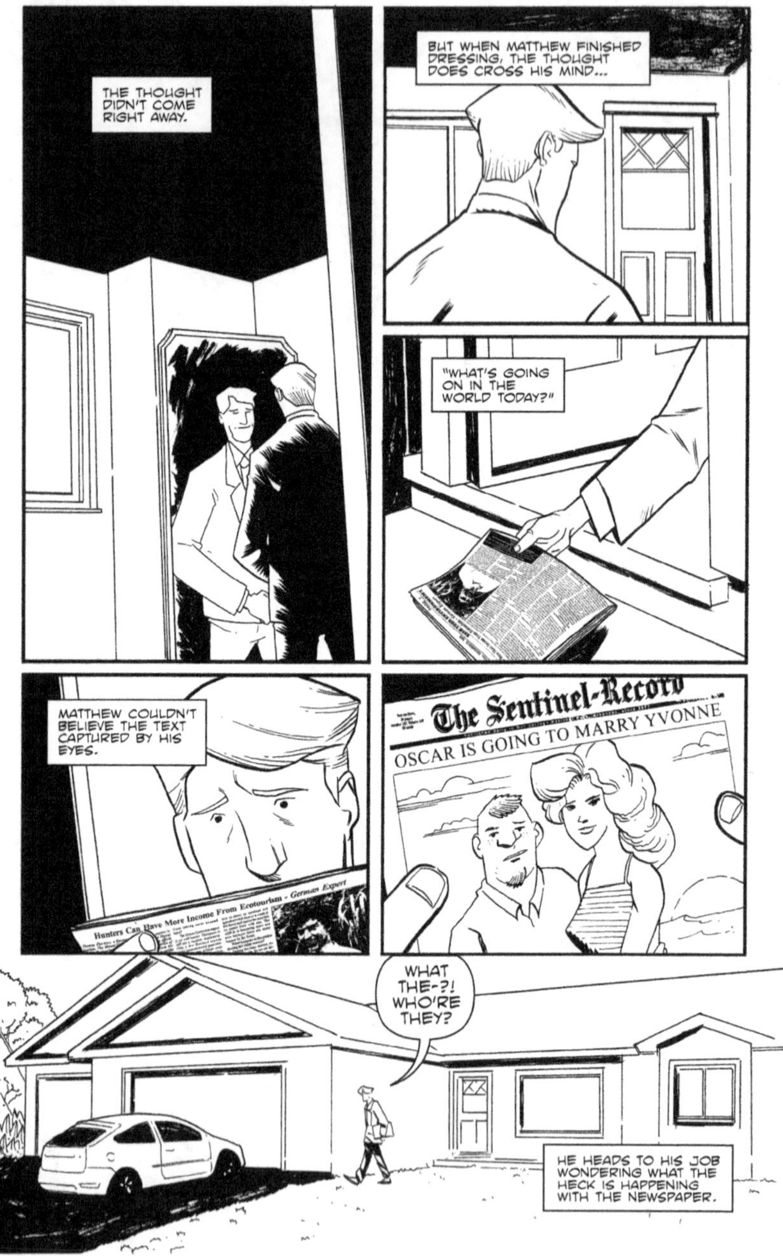

THE THOUGHT DIDN'T COME RIGHT AWAY.
BUT WHEN MATTHEW FINISHED DRESSING, THE THOUGHT DOES CROSS HIS MIND...
"WHAT'S GOING ON IN THE WORLD TODAY?"
MATTHEW COULDN'T BELIEVE THE TEXT CAPTURED BY HIS EYES.
Hunters Can Have More Income From Ecotourism - German Expert
The Sentinel-Record
OSCAR IS GOING TO MARRY YVONNE
WHAT THE-?! WHO'RE THEY?
HE HEADS TO HIS JOB WONDERING WHAT THE HECK IS HAPPENING WITH THE NEWSPAPER.

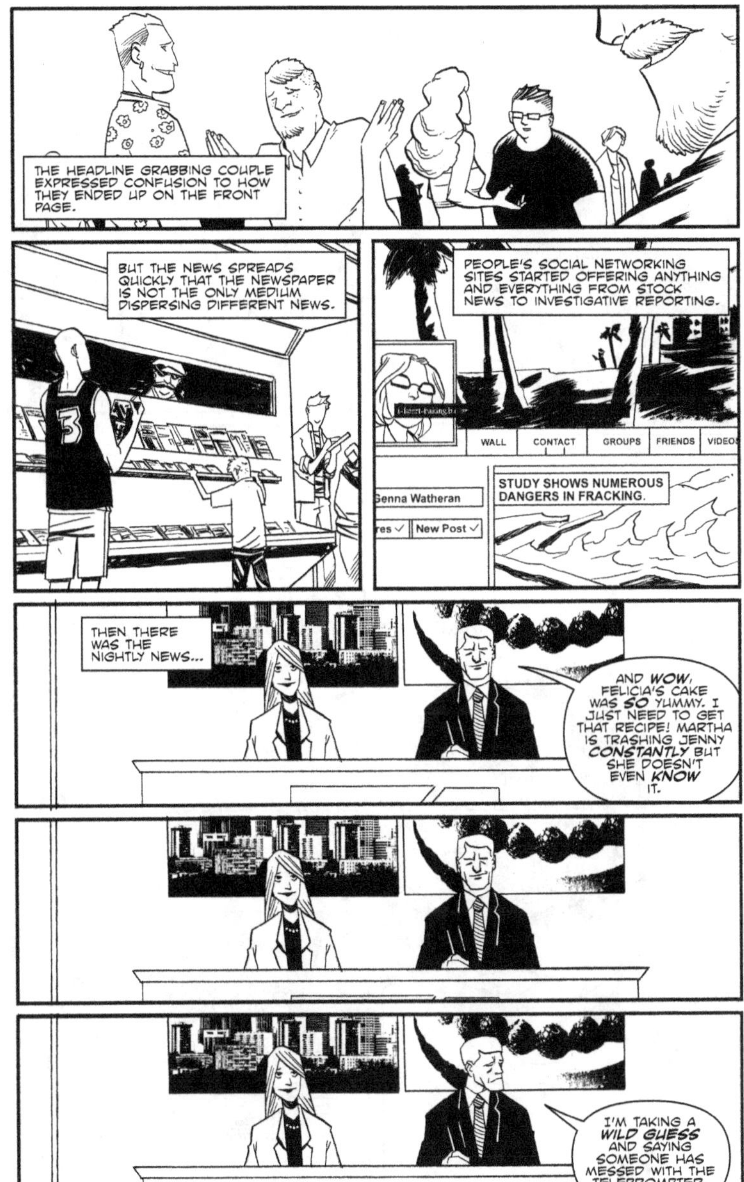

THE HEADLINE GRABBING COUPLE EXPRESSED CONFUSION TO HOW THEY ENDED UP ON THE FRONT PAGE.
BUT THE NEWS SPREADS QUICKLY THAT THE NEWSPAPER IS NOT THE ONLY MEDIUM DISPERSING DIFFERENT NEWS.
PEOPLE'S SOCIAL NETWORKING SITES STARTED OFFERING ANYTHING AND EVERYTHING FROM STOCK NEWS TO INVESTIGATIVE REPORTING.
WALL
CONTACT
GROUPS
FRIENDS
VIDEOS
Genna Watheran
res
New Post
STUDY SHOWS NUMEROUS DANGERS IN FRACKING.
THEN THERE WAS THE NIGHTLY NEWS...
AND WOW, FELICIA'S CAKE WAS SO YUMMY. I JUST NEED TO GET THAT RECIPE! MARTHA IS TRASHING JENNY CONSTANTLY BUT SHE DOESN'T EVEN KNOW IT.
I'M TAKING A WILD GUESS AND SAYING SOMEONE HAS MESSED WITH THE TELEPROMPTER.

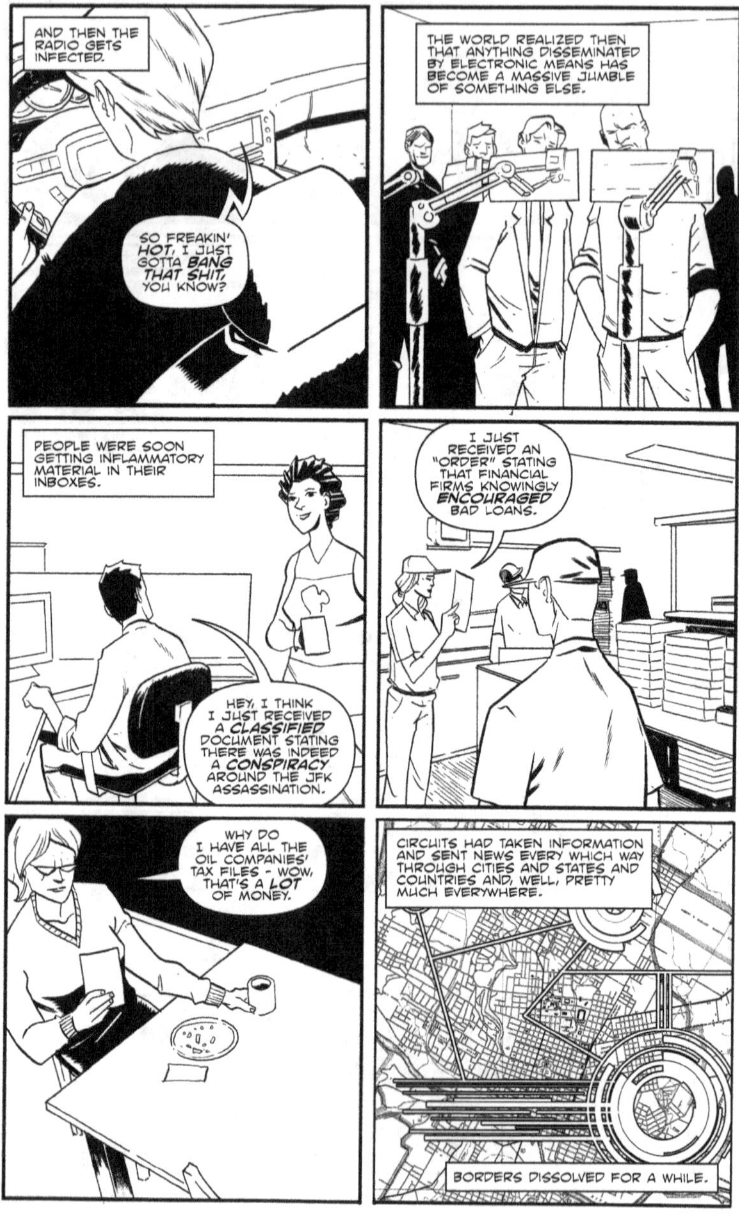

AND THEN THE RADIO GETS INFECTED.
SO FREAKIN' HOT, I JUST GOTTA BANG THAT SHIT, YOU KNOW?
THE WORLD REALIZED THEN THAT ANYTHING DISSEMINATED BY ELECTRONIC MEANS HAS BECOME A MASSIVE JUMBLE OF SOMETHING ELSE.
PEOPLE WERE SOON GETTING INFLAMMATORY MATERIAL IN THEIR INBOXES.
HEY, I THINK I JUST RECEIVED A CLASSIFIED DOCUMENT STATING THERE WAS INDEED A CONSPIRACY AROUND THE JFK ASSASSINATION.
I JUST RECEIVED AN "ORDER" STATING THAT FINANCIAL FIRMS KNOWINGLY ENCOURAGED BAD LOANS.
WHY DO I HAVE ALL THE OIL COMPANIES' TAX FILES - WOW, THAT'S A LOT OF MONEY.
CIRCUITS HAD TAKEN INFORMATION AND SENT NEWS EVERY WHICH WAY THROUGH CITIES AND STATES AND COUNTRIES AND, WELL, PRETTY MUCH EVERYWHERE.
BORDERS DISSOLVED FOR A WHILE.

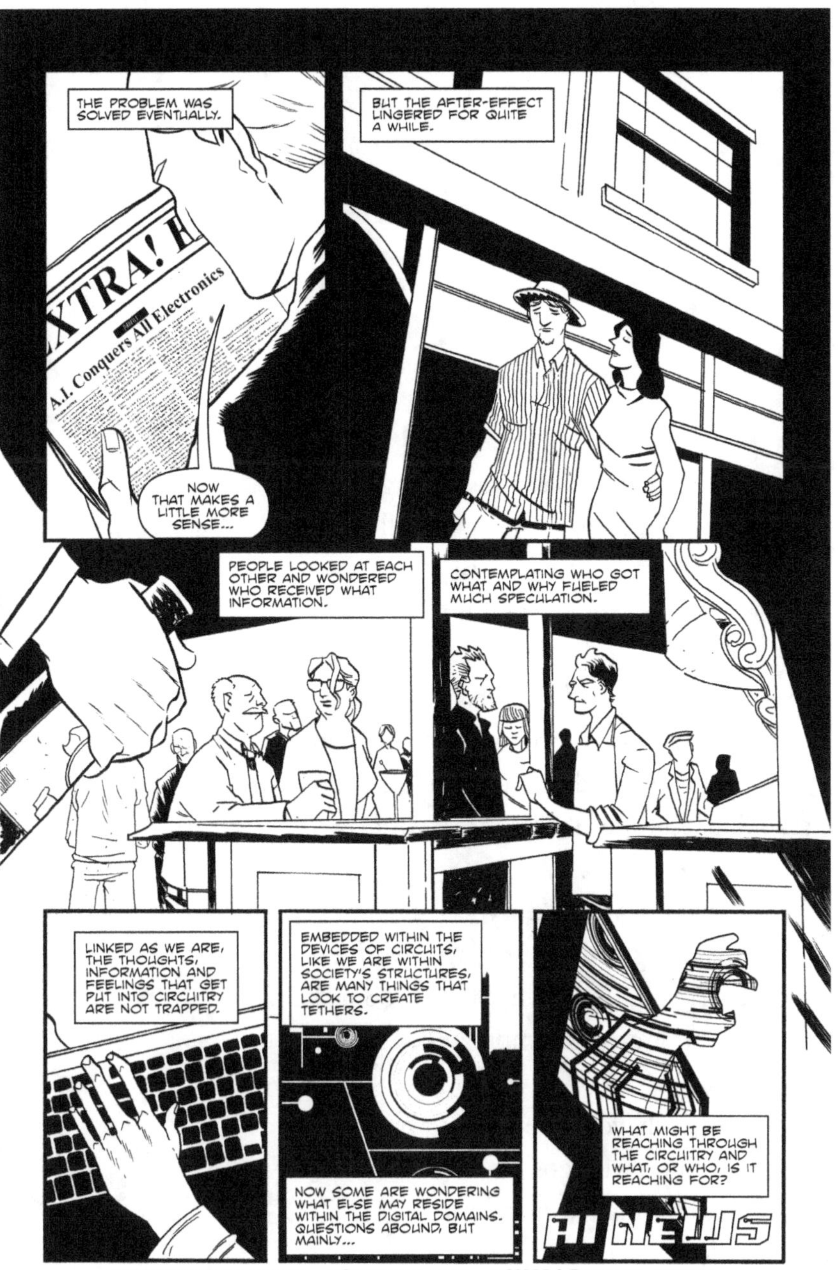

STORY BY PATRICK MCEVOY   ART BY RYAN CODY   LETTERS BY RACHEL DEERING

Window Seat

ALFRED FOURNIER

When word came it was time to say goodbye
to you, Sis, I booked a window seat flight,
so I might watch earth grow small
as the plane rose into generous blue.

I wondered what had changed. For twenty years,
defying each gloomy prognosis, you'd beamed
at every family wedding, your garden flourished,
grandkids scattered smiles across your lawn.

Thought about what I'd say, as sunbathing clouds
shadowed the ground, but arrived wordless
to discover you, radiant, in a living room chair,
family near. I took the empty beside you.

Beyond speech, you gave me your hand,
light as a cloud with gossamer skin.
Your eyes illuminated every space
in our silence, made words obsolete.

Family rattled their trivial prattle.
The Pistons had won, did you see on TV?
Any topic better than *this* topic. I winced,
but you smiled from some airy place.

Later at the airport, I marveled how fearlessly
you'd embraced life and could gratefully let go.
Peering out, saw you on the tarmac, luggageless,
your unbuttoned coat drawn up by a gust of air.

November; The Skier; The Subway

DAVE HEALY

November

The sagging jack-o-lantern
frozen thawed refrozen
its once-fierce visage rendered toothless.

The bony maple
leaves lying beneath it
like a red jacket slipped off
on a too-warm afternoon.

The backyard pond
skinned unskinned reskinned
in the fickle not-still-fall
not-yet-winter weather.

The taste of an apple
handed from a blushing bride
to a guileless husband
as they gaze upon a garden gone to seed.

The Skier

Danny Crocker was a bronzed god
who ruled the waterfront at
Big Trout Lake Bible Camp.

When he swam the butterfly
the water parted before him
like a staff-split sea.

Pulled behind Bob Wallberg's boat
he started on two skis
like any other mortal

but as their wide circle
brought them back in front of us
he casually flicked one off

and took another lap
carving the water like a snake
his chiseled body leaning over the lake

at an impossible angle
his single ski sending up a nimbus
of spray that stretched toward heaven.

Another circle brought him
back to us yet again
and now he did the impossible

shedding his remaining ski
as if he were shaking

the dust from his sandals

then walking on the water
just another miracle
for our now believing eyes.

The Subway

On the 5 train to Brooklyn
the seats full
a dozen standing
most wired to their screens
when suddenly
from the middle of the car
a man began to speak.

His was an oft-told tale:
how he lost his wife
turned to drink
hit bottom
but now by the grace of God
is slowly climbing back up.

The windup completed
we waited for the pitch:
anything you can do to help
something to get me back on my feet.

But he fooled us with a changeup
asking only that we say a prayer for him
and when he got off at Nostrand

and disappeared into the crowd
his request hung in the air
every seam visible
as we plunged on in darkness.

EMULSION

TERRY HALL BODINE

Chickens love dust baths. They dig shallow basins,
spread their wings, and use feet to kick dust
into their feathers. This trick helps chickens
maintain proper insulation and wards off parasites.

Prairies provoke dust storms. Self-centered winds score
acres-long troughs into fields, grit gusted to form grainy
sepia clouds achingly devoid of rain. The house,
the tractor, the haystacks stain, dun-colored and dull.

I dig my heels into the barnyard, use my feet to scuff
dust up around my ankles. Cool as silk, the silt clings
to my calves. With a fingertip I trace a crooked line
along my leg, white where the dirt erases instead

of dark like a stocking's seam--life exposed again
as the photo negative of dreams.

Remember

ERIN BLOCK

Remember the heat of standing by a wood shed
in slant autumn sun
When all the warmth has come inside
like the mice
like the stray cats
like the pack rats
who'd steal jewelry if you had it.

And when the snow comes
and someone,
but never you,
wins the canyon bet on first fall
Remember how it rained
once in the whole month of August
And how it felt like falling
in love with a man again
After enough years
you can't remember how it started
Like all the fights you made love for afterwards.

When the doe walks slow
pass-grazing on jamesia and maple
And you need just one more step
for the shoulder to open the world

wide like a high plains sunrise
Remember how to be patient
with your finger on that trigger
Like your cat sitting stand on a vole
How he takes no chances
because in the real world
those'll leave you hungry
or worse.

And when the mountain freezes
Like a snowshoe hare under spruce
Remember how the soil was once so soft
when you put your old dog in the ground
no one could hear the tears fall.

BUYING THE REAL: THE 1950S

DAVID RADAVICH

I don't really remember
who we were. It was another
time, when families were created
on TV and we all became
what we saw, or tried to.

Who knew what a father is,
or was, apart from those scenes
arriving home from work,
suit only slightly disheveled
and smiles in every dimension?

Mother was somehow never
too busy, the meal not a burden,
waist slender, breasts raised,
the neighbors all on good terms.

That much I remember.

Somewhere there's the ghost
of myself who couldn't look away
at the child beaten in his room,
the slammed door, the car
ripped open and sped away.

Not to mention the late, late
nights of absence, somewhere
at a bar, or maybe just a cliff
with the top rolled down
and nothing bright to look at.

The songs seemed to open
every heart to worlds
that couldn't be, love, just
a cigarette, a Corvette,
a fleshed thigh away from bliss.

In the end, I learned
anything was a purchase away
from being what was real.

Strawberries

MARY DIXON

Strawberries are the feasible angst that summer brings
Their crackling seeds catch in the teeth
My husband covers the bed
With mesh wires to thwart the blackbirds
Still encaged in the thriving
Simply pasted into cordiality
He seems to weave a wonderful coating
Protecting the berries some sour

We find ourselves born into light or darkness
In the shame of night and the glory of day
Without creation without explanation
Clinging to vines like berries

Without the wood-gnawing beaver
In the creasing of rivers as a slowly dying poplar
Is gutted by those relentless creatures
A damn to construct a world of protection
In domes accessible only from under water
Skeleton trees fall to the flood and dam up their roaring stream

Closely gathering sprigs some even blooming
No discretion between cottonwood or elm or even the dogwood
All an object to appetites not for food but for shelter

The cage for strawberries losing significance

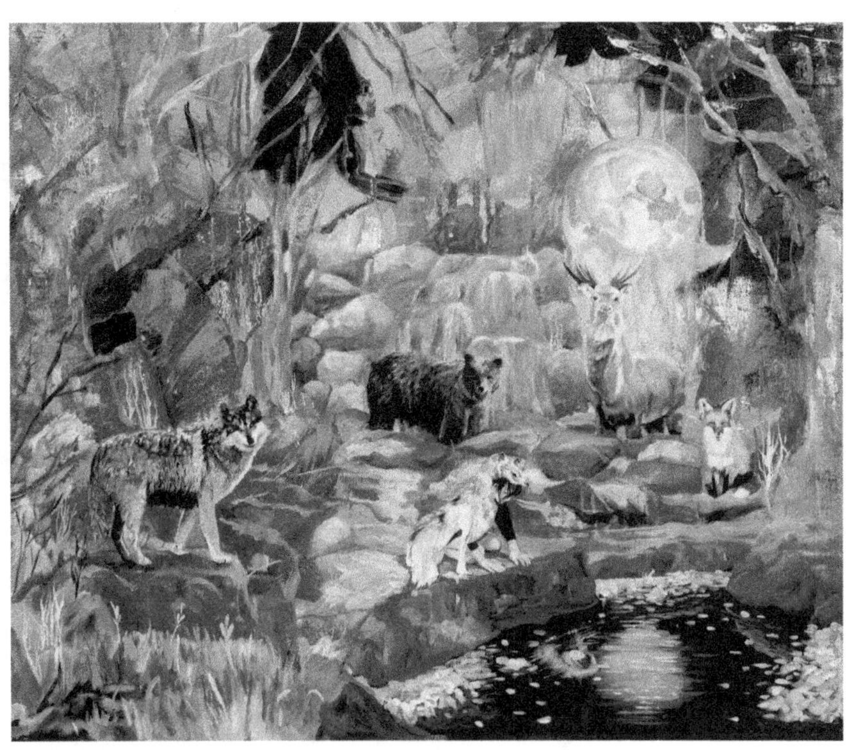

"Disguise," acrylic, 24 x 36 inches
Hyeseon Kim

The Event

KURT OLSSON

That which
cannot happen
which
will not happen
which must
not happen
not here not
now not ever
the impossible
the unimaginable
factorless
unpredicted & unpredictable
& secretly wished for.

HELICOPTERS, HURRICANES, CAR WRECKS!

JONATHAN MUNDELL

Don't bullshit me, poet.
No one cares about your clever en
jambments, metaphors, moon
light and slinking cigarettes—put
the cigarette in the mouth of the moon,
and light, poet. If there's
tears, let them be your reader's when
they tear
the page in two, cursing the brother
lying at the side of your poem dead,
metallic earth
clicking inside the shells of your
machine gun words. Swing
a vile cock or whatever you have
that spits, and
be vile be vile be vile lick
the ground of the ashes, sniff
for any trace of what it is to be—
give me a helicopter, hurricane,
car wreck poet, the sky filled your
mouth and couldn't breathe type
poet, slit-wrist poet, laugh out loud

poet, make me laugh at death
and the moon the moon the moon
inside beads of sweat, laugh
poet, again again again click
the stone in your lighter, and when
does it even matter
appears below your smoke pen,
poet, write
so fast the ink on the page burns
your heart your lungs your skin

Lost Falcon

DONALD ILLICH

I wear a glove for the falcon,
for it to bring back prey,
and squawk its delight
we are partners in the world.

It's been many years,
though, since the predator
has returned to my hand.
I haven't given up hope.

I keep my glove on at all times,
even when I'm eating steak
and have trouble holding the plate,
or when I'm the best man

at a wedding, fumbling the ring
because I can't grip small items.
Sometimes I'll raise my arm
at almost any moment, in hopes

the falcon detects my presence.
In the theater they complain,
or throw popcorn, candy at me,
while during the National Anthem

people misunderstand my "salute,"
yell I'm disgracing the flag,
threaten to fight me outside.
I can't stop searching for my comrade.

It's alone out there in the wind,
seeking the right hand, tempted
by many others, but knowing
we share a rapport, a mental bond.

It'll rush toward me like diamonds
shooting through the air, and my mailed
glove will be ready to seize it,
bring it back down to the Earth.

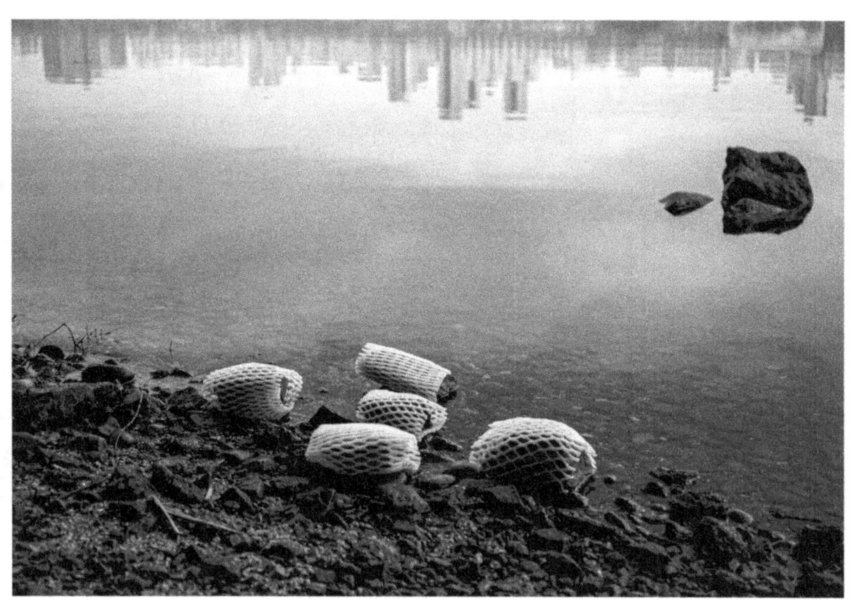

"Styrofoam Rocks," photograph
Hyeseon Kim

Benjamin Litoff has a masters degree from Georgetown in communications and a bachelors in sociology from Ithaca College. He has studied writing under Fred Wilcox, Mary Beth O'Connor, and Michael Long. Currently, he lives in Washington DC with his wife, Dana.

Caren Messing writes poetry, short stories, and essays. Her essay "A Modicum of Comfort" appeared in the anthology "America, September 11th The Courage to Give" (MJF Books/Fine Communications, Conari Press 2001). Her short short story "In The Studio" is included in the third of the special issues of Asylum Magazine on Comics and Mental Health (Autumn 2015). She is also a vocalist, actor & filmmaker and lives in NYC.

C.W. Bigelow lived in nine northern states, both east and west, after receiving his B.A. in English from Colorado State University and before moving south to the Charlotte NC area. His short stories and poems have appeared in *The Flexible Persona, Literally Stories, Compass Magazine, FishFood Magazine, Five2One, Crack the Spine, Sick Lit Magazine, Anthology: River Tales* by Zimbell House Publishing, *Midway Journal, Scarlet Leaf Review, Poydras Review, Cleaning Up Glitter, The Blue Mountain Review, Glassworks, Blood & Bourbon, The Courtship of Winds, Backchannels*, among many others, with stories forthcoming in *Drunk Monkeys* and *Good Works Review*.

william c. crawford is a photographer based in Winston-Salem, NC. He invented Forensic Foraging, a throwback, minimalist approach for modern digital photographers. His new book, *Crawdaddy Chases the Money Shot*, is available on Amazon.com

Wayne Bowen was born in 1949 in Fayetteville, Arkansas. When he was twelve years old, his family moved to Amarillo, Texas. There he attended junior high school, high school, and community college. In the fall of 1970, he entered Abilene Christian College. Halfway through the spring semester, he dropped out for financial reasons and soon found himself in the United States Army, which sent him to Germany. After his honorable discharge from active duty, he attended The University of Texas at Austin, where he majored in German. After completing a BA and an MA degree, he taught high school, first in Port Arthur and then back in Austin, where he has lived ever since. When he retired from teaching, he began to write, mostly fiction. He does not always find writing fun, but he does always find it satisfying. To him, that is a good reason to continue writing.

Patrick Cabello Hansel is the author of the poetry collections *The Devouring Land* (Main Street Rag Publishing) and *Quitting Time* (forthcoming from Atmosphere Press). He has published poems and prose in over 65 journals, including *subprimal, Ilanot Review, Ash & Bones,* and *Lunch Ticket.* His novella "Searching" was serialized in 33 issues of *The Alley News*. He has been nominated for a Pushcart Prize and received awards from the Loft Literary Center and the MN State Arts Board. He is the editor of *The Phoenix of Phillips* literary magazine, a new journal for and by the people of the most diverse neighborhood in Minneapolis.

Robert Harrington writes and teaches English in Florida.

David S. Rubenstein is an American writer, photographer, poet, and painter. His short stories have appeared in numerous journals and have been nominated twice for the Pushcart prize. David's photographs appear in *Writing Disorder* where he was featured artist, and several additional publications. D-M Farm is on permanent display in the Village of Montgomery town hall. Three photo prints on metal were displayed at the 2019 "Exposure" show at the SCJF. Photo "White Stillness" on metal to appear in Wisconsin ArtsWest 41 show. His poem "High Place" appears in *The Write Launch*. An interview with the author appears in *Midwest Gothic* Jan 2018. A collection of his short stories can be found on Kobo at https://www.kobo.com/us/en/ebook/piasa-and-other-stories.

Hilary Wheelan Remley was raised in the suburbs of Atlanta, Georgia. She currently lives in Alexandria, Virginia. She is finishing her MA at UAlbany. Her work has previously been published in *Prometheus Dreaming* and *Meat for Tea: The Valley Review*.

Brodie Lowe was awarded the Elizabeth Boatwright Coker Fellowship in Fiction by the South Carolina Academy of Authors. He was a semi-finalist of The Nancy Zafris Short-Story Fellowship. He was a finalist of the Ron Rash Award in Fiction and Still: The Journal's Literary Contest in Fiction. His stories have been published in *The Broad River Review*, *Mystery Tribune*, *The Bark Magazine*, *Nebo: A Literary Journal*, *Antithesis Journal*, *Eastern Iowa Review*, *The Windhover*, and elsewhere. He holds a BA in English from Western Carolina University.

James Hartman's fiction appears in *Blue Fifth Review*, *December*, *Raleigh Review*, *Gris-Gris*, and *New World Writing*, among others. His story, "A Junior Whopper, Please, With Cheese," was nominated for a Pushcart Prize and Best Small Fictions. His scholarly work is featured in *The Hemingway Review*. He lives in York, Pennsylvania.

Richard Nickel is an artist, educator, and writer who has exhibited both nationally and internationally. He has been published in several books on contemporary ceramics and in art journals. As a designer, Nickel has created posters for Crafted Indie Arts and Crafts Market, a cover illustration for *Studio Potter*, ceramic awards for Skutt Kilns, illustrations for *Alt Daily*, and animations for WHRO HealthBeat. As a ceramic sculptor, he has pieces in numerous private collections. Nickel has designed and painted murals in Rochester, New York; Niagara Falls, New York; Norfolk, Virginia; and Virginia Beach, Virginia.

Ethan Cunningham is a creative wanderer. He holds an MFA from Boston University. His short works and photography have appeared in *Fiction365*, *Forth Magazine*, *Three Line Poetry*, *Agave Magazine*, among others. He has also worked on several award-winning short documentaries featuring international non-profit endeavors: *Operation International: Ivory Coast*, *Rally for Rangers*, and *Darkhad Valley*. Ethan lives in California with his wife and cats.

Laura Bonazzoli is a freelance writer and editor living on the coast of Maine. Her poetry has appeared in dozens of literary magazines and in anthologies, and is forthcoming in the *Naugatuck River Review*, the *Northern New England Review*, and *The Lyric*, among others. She has also published short stories and essays. She is on the web at laurabonazzoli.com and on Instagram at laura.bonazzoli.

Sara Gilbert is a third year Ph.D. student in fiction at Oklahoma State University with a secondary emphasis in contemporary Irish literature. She has an MFA in Fiction from American College Dublin in Ireland, and an MA in English Literature from the University of Texas at San Antonio. Her writing has been featured in *Minerva Rising's The Keeping Room*, *Cathexis Northwest Press*, *Havik Literary Journal*, *Jenny*, *Meat for Tea: The Valley Review*, and the *Santa Clara Review*. Her work tends to focus on behavioral psychology and is based in places her own travels have taken her.

Jill Bronfman is a professor, lawyer, non-profit worker, and parent. Her work has been accepted for publication in *Rougarou*, *Ruminate Magazine*, *The Write Launch*, *The Decadent Review*, *The Halcyone*, *82 Review*, *The Passed Note*, *Storgy*, *Verbal*, *Kallisto Gaia*, *Main Street Rag*, *High Desert*, *Flying Ketchup*, *Carcosa*, *Genre: Urban Arts*, *Ripples* *in Space, Mothers Always Write, Talking Writing, Coffin Bell Journal, Flock, Wanderlust Journal, Quiet Lightening,* and law and technical books and periodicals. She has performed her work in Poets in the Parks, The Basement Series, and LitQuake, and had her story about a middle-aged robot produced as a podcast.

Terry Savoie has had more than four hundred poems published over the past four decades. These include ones in *APR, Poetry* (Chicago), *Ploughshares, North American Review, Sonora Review, American Journal of Poetry* and *The Iowa Review* as well as recent or forthcoming issues of *North Dakota Quarterly, One, America, Chiron Review,* and *Tar River Poetry* among others. A selection, "Reading Sunday," won the Bright Hill Chapbook Competition and was published in the spring of 2018.

Rick Christman is the author of *Falling in Love at the End of the World* (New Rivers Press), fiction, and *Searching for Mozart* (Brighthorse Books), poetry. He lives in the South Carolina Low Country.

Steven Deutsch. After a glamorous childhood in Brownsville, Brooklyn, Steve (and his wife, Karen), settled in State College, PA. They have one son—the guitarist for the avant-garde group, Gang Gang Dance. Over the last two years, Steve's work has appeared in more than two dozen print and online journals. He was twice nominated for the Pushcart Prize. He is the current poetry editor for *Centered Magazine*. Steve's chapbook, *Perhaps You Can*, was published by Kelsay Books in 2019. His full-length poetry book, *The Persistence of Memory*, has just been published by Kelsay.

Frank Dullaghan is an Irish writer with four collections published by Cinnamon Press (UK). His most recent collection is *Lifting the Latch* (2018). His poems are published widely, including in *Cyphers, London Magazine, New Welsh Review, Nimrod, Orbis, Poetry Review,* and *Rattle.*

Jack Stewart was educated at the University of Alabama and Emory University. From 1992-95 he was a Brittain Fellow at The Georgia Institute of Technology. Jack's work has appeared in *Poetry, The American Literary Review, The Dark Horse Review, The Southern Humanities Review,* and other journals and anthologies, most recently in *New Welsh Reader* and *Image.* His book, *No Reason,* is forthcoming from the Poeima Poetry Series. Jack lives in Coconut Creek, Florida.

Patrick McEvoy is a former writer and editor for several sports publications. Patrick has have had stories included in various comic book anthologies such as *Emanata, Uncanny Adventures, Indie Comics Quarterly,* and *GuruKitty's Once Upon a Time and Gateway to Beyond.* A short story has also appeared on Akashic Books' website. In addition, short plays Patrick wrote were chosen to be performed at the Players Theatre in New York as part of their various festivals (Sex, NYC, and BOO) in 2013, 2014, 2015, 2016, and 2019. And a short play was accepted into Emerging Artists Theatre New Works series in 2020. His photography has also been exhibited with the Greenpoint Gallery and *Tiny Seed Literary Journal.*

Alfred Fournier is an entomologist and community volunteer living in Phoenix, Arizona. He coordinates poetry workshops for a local nonprofit. His poetry and prose have appeared in *The New Verse News,* Plainsongs, *Lunch Ticket, The Main Street Rag,* and elsewhere. He has work forthcoming in *The Perch Magazine.*

Dave Healy is a retired college teacher, administrator, and editor. He edited the *Writing Center Journal, Public Art Review,* and the *Park Bugle* newspaper.

Terry Hall Bodine is a graduate of the College of William & Mary in Virginia. Recent publication credits include *Common Ground Review, Heirlock,* and *The Raw Art Review.* Terry lives in Lynchburg with her husband, Bill, and works with student life at the University of Lynchburg.

Erin Block works as a librarian and freelance writer. She is the author of two books, *The View from Coal Creek* and *By a Thread*. Her work has been published in *The Rumpus, The Columbia Review, Guernica and Gray's Sporting Journal*, among others. She lives in a cabin in the Rocky Mountains of Colorado where she hunts, fishes, forages, and gardens.

David Radavich's latest narrative collection, *American Abroad: An Epic of Discovery* (2019), is a companion volume to his earlier *American Bound: An Epic for Our Time* (2007). Recent lyric collections are *Middle-East Mezze* (2011) and *The Countries We Live* (2014). His plays have been performed across the U.S. and in Europe.

Mary Marie Dixon, a visual artist and poet, has published creative and academic works in various periodicals and anthologies, and a collection of poetry, *Eucharist, Enter the Sacred Way*, Franciscan University Press, 2008. Her focus is on women's spirituality and the mystics, combined with the Great Plains and the spiritual power of nature. She has exhibited her visual work and accompanying poetry in galleries and explores the visual and poetic intersection in her creative life. She loves stars, sunrises, and sunsets on the open plains! https://www.facebook.com/pages/Mary-Marie-Dixon/104361173006800.

Hyeseon Kim is a senior attending North London Collegiate School Jeju in South Korea. She is currently preparing a portfolio to attend university. Her other hobbies include contemporary dance, piano, and soccer.

Kurt Olsson's work has appeared in a wide variety of publications, including *Poetry, Southern Review, FIELD*, and *The New Republic*. Second collection of poetry, *Burning Down Disneyland* (Gunpowder

Press), was selected by Thomas Lux as the winner of the 2016 Barry Spacks Poetry Award.

Jonathan Mundell's work has appeared in *The Closed Eye Open*. He currently lives and teaches in South Florida.

Donald Illich has published poetry in journals such as the *Iowa Review*, *Fourteen Hills*, and *Cold Mountain Review*. He won Honorable Mention in the Washington Prize book contest. He recently published a book, *Chance Bodies* (The Word Works, 2018).

SUBMISSION INFORMATION

New Plains Review accepts original work in poetry, prose, and visual art. Submission information and editorial guidelines are accessible through the website.

ORDERING INFORMATION

Pricing for current and back issues is available through Amazon.

www.ingramcontent.com/pod-product-compliance
Lightning Source LLC
Chambersburg PA
CBHW061515050726
47593CB00002B/574